The
PERCEPT

Manish Vohra

V&S PUBLISHERS

Published by:

V&S PUBLISHERS

F-2/16, Ansari Road, Daryaganj, New Delhi-110002
☎ 011-23240026, 011-23240027 • *Fax:* 011-23240028
Email: info@vspublishers.com • *Website:* www.vspublishers.com

Branch : Hyderabad
5-1-707/1, Brij Bhawan (Beside Central Bank of India Lane)
Bank Street, Koti, Hyderabad - 500 095.
☎ 040-24737290.
E-mail: vspublishershyd@gmail.com

Follow us on:

For any assistance sms **VSPUB** to **56161**
All books available at **www.vspublishers.com**

© **Copyright: Author**
ISBN 978-93-815889-5-6
Edition 2013

Printed at : Param Offseters, Okhla, New Delhi-110020

Dedication

I dedicate this book to
all my readers.

Acknowledgements

Life has blessed me with many teachers and guiding influences who have, in their own ways, each contributed to the writing of this book. I would like to thank my parents Narindar and Indra whose unconditional love I am blessed with.

My special thanks to Sahil who trusted his instincts and made this endeavor possible and the editorial team from V& S Publishers for their valuable inputs.

My thanks to my wife Shilpa for her unsparing support and also to my children Gaurav and Aditi.

I express my deep sense of gratitude to my readers whose enthusiastic response and positive feedback made this book possible.

The Background....

Sudesh Kapoor had just appeared for his XII grade exams (junior college) and was dreading the day his results would be announced. It was not that he had fared badly in any subject but he knew he was average and his score would also be average. Nobody understood that he didn't like to study. Sudesh was average in sports and really bad at music and painting and there was no way out but to study hard and do well in exams. Despite being average at everything, Sudesh had dreams of being very successful in life. He dreamt that one day he would do things never done before.

Dream Big

Well one shouldn't bother about the future because it comes soon enough and very soon came the day when the results of the XIIth grade were to be announced. Sudesh had woken up at 3 a.m. because of tension, he didn't want to disappoint his parents but there was nothing he could do. There was nothing in his control and he had done his best. Sudesh's father Ravi Kapoor had also woken up early and was pacing

up and down the large balcony attached to his room and his mother Divya Kapoor was pretending to be asleep but the truth was she hadn't slept even a wink the whole night. Sudesh's parents were doctors, and very successful at that. Sudesh's father was a well established ENT surgeon who travelled all over the world presenting his case papers and his mother was a pediatrician. She dealt with very small children. Both his parents were very well known and Sudesh often wondered that when his parents were so brilliant how come he was very average.

At 9 a.m. that day Sudesh drove down to the junior college with his parents to see the results. He had wished his parents not accompany him. But his dad insisted on coming along. On the way to the notice board where the results were displayed Sudesh spotted all his friends dressed in their finest clothes. Sudesh stopped to chat with his friend Ramesh Tiwary while his parents made their way to the notice board.

The story begins....

Ramesh told me he had got 86% marks and that his parents were disappointed because they expected him to get over 92% at least. I told him if I got anywhere close to even 80% I would demand a new iPad and a new cell phone from my parents. Ramesh looked at me and nodded and said.

"I don't think you even need to study or do anything in life. Your parents are loaded".

I nodded back.

How could I tell my close friend Ramesh that I had dreams of being very successful? But there was nothing in particular I wanted to pursue because I was average at everything. Soon enough I felt my father's hand on my shoulders and one look at his face told me that the news was not good. My mother whispered in my ears – "You've got 69%".

She didn't say anything more but her tone reassured me.

The ride back home was difficult. Dad was in his silent mood and mom didn't have the courage to say anything in front of dad. When we had almost reached home, dad said – "we'll discuss your future in the evening".

But it was comforting because I knew the discussion would be in the living room and grandpa always had his drink in the evening in the living room. So the discussion would be in the presence of grandpa and mom, and both were always on my side. My grandpa was a famous writer and had done very well for himself. Although my grandma was no more, I always felt the romance in his books had kept her alive.

I had everything an 18 year old would want from doting parents, money to spend with my friends, yet at every result time I was humbled. I had to pretend I didn't study hard enough before my friends. Often I repeated what grandpa always told me – 'Marks don't mean anything, a number will not decide whether you will succeed or fail in life.' But the truth was in India a number decided your entrance into a medical or engineering college. So your percentage did decide your future. I wondered why grandpa could never see that.

I had about 6 hours to prepare for the meeting with my family and I thought it was best to prepare a defence strategy.

So I prepared a list of reasons why I didn't do well.

The questions were out of the syllabus.

The examiners did not understand what I wrote.

May be there was a mistake and we should send the papers for re-evaluation. But I know in my heart the marks I had got were exactly what I had deserved, and that I was just average.

I spent the next few hours brooding about what I should do now and what the future would hold for me. I was sure I would pursue whatever my parents asked me to pursue as they had my best interests in their mind. I was a little spoilt because my parents always got me everything I wanted but I was not a rebel. I knew I would do exactly what my parents would want me to do.

Well, it was 7.30 p.m. and I knew I was expected to be in the living room. It was time for my future to be decided. I went to the living room and sat quietly not daring to look my dad in the face. I looked around and saw my grandpa, he didn't care two hoots, he was too busy with his drink and enjoying the soft music on the stereo. Mom was not present and so I figured, whatever dad had to say to me had mom's approval.

And then dad said, "There's something you must know".

I took a deep breath not knowing what would happen next.

"Your grandpa and I both were very average".

I thought okay; thank God they are in a mood to ignore my poor performance. The most famous writer of his time and a very famous surgeon were average. Well thank God they love me so much that they will lie to me on my face.

My father smiled as if he had read my thoughts and said.

"You don't understand. There's something we've hidden from you. There's something you must know."

I wondered what the family could have hidden from me.

"Well", my dad continued – "your grandpa was a struggling writer for a long time until he met Swami Sutradev".

"I know that" I said – "grandpa reveres Swami Sutradev".

"Well" dad said – "what you don't know is that grandpa became a monk for one year and spent one year at the Jan

Bhumi monastery under Swami Sutradev". What, I almost felt knocked out; my own grandpa was a monk?

And dad continued – "I continued his legacy and spent one year as a monk at the same monastery under Swami Sutradev".

I felt completely smashed, my own grandpa and dad were monks for one year and I didn't know.

My dad explained – "Under some traditions it is possible to become a monk for only one or two years but you have to keep absolute secrecy, you have to take a vow that you will never reveal the secrets, which is why you don't know anything about that one year of my life".

The question now is – "Will you continue the family legacy?"

I didn't know what to say. I had thought my dad would send me abroad for schooling. That was the worst case scenario but this was a blow I was not ready for. Was I willing to leave behind everything and become a monk for one year?

What crap I thought – I had just started making friends with girls and also started getting attention from girls. If Sushma or Rita found out I was headed for a monastery what would they think? What would all my friends think? Thank God where I would go for one year would be a secret.

There's no way I could afford to have any of my friends know I was headed for a monastery. I decided I would tell my friends I'm taking a vacation. I was not sure what dad would be telling my friends.

I asked my dad for some time to think things over.

"It's your life and your decision; you will not be forced into anything. You can choose to pursue anything you want". – Dad replied.

I knew he meant it. I would have the freedom to do anything with my life. I felt I didn't want freedom, I wanted direction. I wanted to succeed and I wanted someone to show me how.

As I paced up and down in my room avoiding all calls from my friends, I decided to study the facts. Both grandpa and dad were extremely successful and both of them had become monks for one year. Grandpa and dad both claimed to me in private to be average. There was something in that monastery and I could not put my finger on it. There was something they learnt in that monastery which resulted in this transformation. I had met Swami Sutradev and he had always been very kind and gentle with me.

I thought this was because of the large donations dad and my grandpa gave to the monastery. I never thought the monks

could have given my dad and grandpa anything. Evidently the truth was the other way around. Those poor monks had given my family the formula for success. I felt very small indeed. The world is a very funny place and everything is not as it seems. Everything I had perceived to be true was suddenly not as true

as I had earlier believed.

'What would the monks teach me in one year?' I wondered. I knew all the funny breathing exercises called pranayama and

     The Perceptionist

had been compulsorily doing them for the last five years, if I missed a day my pocket money would be deducted. I could not afford any deduction in my pocket money as I loved to treat my friends and my friends doted on me. My world revolved around my friends, playing with my friends was the only thing I found pleasurable. And now I must leave behind all my friends for one year for what?

If those monks try to teach me breathing exercises I would tell them to compress the course from one year to six months because I already knew all the breathing exercises. I knew a little bit about meditation also but didn't practice it.

TRUE FRIENDS ARE HARD TO COME BY.

So I decided this was the best course of action – I would land up in the monastery, and after some time I would question all the monks about what they knew and whether the syllabus could be compressed from one year to one month. Then I would convince them to let me go home in one month instead of one year. I decided I would convince the abbot Swami Sutradev that an 18 year old should not be in a monastery. If this failed I had plan B, I

would tell the abbot that I would come to the monastery for one month every year for 12 years thus completing my one year in the monastery. If this failed I had plan C, I would convince them that I was indisciplined and should not spend time in the monastery because others might also become indisciplined.

I figured there was no way I could have my parent's love, comforts of home, my friends and enjoy success at the same time. I could have them all but spread over different time periods. I understood sacrifices had to be made for success and my grandpa and dad had made those sacrifices.

So even though I had plans to escape from the monastery within 1 month there was a part in me which told me I should give it my best shot. This could be the one year which will define my entire future. But there was another part in me which told me, who the hell goes to a monastery? I figured only losers. Life is beautiful. Do these monks ever notice it? Every sun rise is more spectacular than the previous one. You only need to look at the clouds in the sky to know for sure God is an artist. I often wondered how come everybody has a different face. The artist does not have much to play

around with two eyes, one nose, two ears and hair and he keeps churning up infinite possibilities and it's not as if he cannot repeat the face he does so in the case of twins.

I was not dead sure I wanted to go to the monastery, but this, was the first time I experienced 'peer pressure', my dad and grandpa had done it, why couldn't I? Although they did not say it I knew my dad and grandpa would be disappointed if I didn't go. These are the two people who love me most and if they feel an uncomfortable life of one year in a monastery is good for me then it must be so. But I did feel that they are nuts. Who goes to a monastery at the age of 18? May be successful people are nuts, at least the sacrifices they make are abnormal I thought.

So I thought I would consider the pros and cons and come at an appropriate decision.

The monks were all nice and gentle people so I decided to give them one mark. The food at the monastery is awful so that's minus one and to add to that no cell phones are allowed in the monastery, there are no I phones or I pad allowed, there's no cable TV, no friends and worst of all no girls to speak to.

So as you can see for every plus one mark for the monastery there were at least 10 marks minus. I knew I had total freedom in deciding my destiny and a part of me told me it had already been decided and the next one year I would be a monk at the Jan Bhumi monastery under Swami Sutradev. Life never fails to surprise; it always renders blows you can never expect. By the time you have the answers ready, life changes the questions. I would never have believed the road to success in the material world would lie inside a monastery.

These are people who have renounced the world and the entire world follows them. How can you renounce when nothing is yours anyway? May be one day I would ask Swami Sutradev (the abbot). They say only

God exists and He is one without a second. Everywhere I saw families exist even in animals and birds. In the entire universe I see the concept of family. I decided to ask the abbot how come the Creator decides to create the concept in every living being but the Hindu sacred texts say God is one without a second i.e. He has no family. I realized my mind had moved on from whether I would go to the monastery or not to what I wanted to ask the abbot and whether I would be able to live without the comforts of home.

I wanted what my grandpa and my dad had, it was indefinable and very subtle but they had it. They could see what others could not. My grandpa often said, see through your inner eyes if you see through your senses you will be deceived. I wanted to open my inner eyes and see like the Gods but alas the secrets lay inside a monastery. Soon there was no doubt in my mind I would follow my family legacy.

I hardly slept that night and after a while I was waiting for the morning when I could announce to my parents and grandpa I would follow the family legacy. I would become a monk for one year. My dad's nod of approval meant the world to me and I knew he would be proud of me. The conniving side of my mind was already working on a plan. May be I could convince grandpa to give some extra donations to the monastery and explain to him that the monks badly needed cable TV and music. But there was one hitch; would the Swami Sutradev who was the abbot at the monastery accept cable TV and music? I figured not but I had a plan to tackle him. The monastery ran a school for poor children around the monastery and had a small dispensary to cater to the medical facilities of the poor

villagers who lived in areas around the monastery. So the monastery was always in need of money. May be I could subtly give the abbot a hint that the donations came at a cost and that grandpa may not give a large donation if I was not comfortable at the monastery. Then I remembered what the abbot Swami Sutradev had said once – He said 'the giver should be thankful' because he has an opportunity to collect some good Karmic points and I figured no, there's no way the abbot could be twisted, also if my grandpa found out about my subtle blackmail he could be really upset. Right then I heard my dad's voice in the background and I knew the time had come to face my dad.

"Dad" – I called out.

"Yes sonny boy" my dad replied, I'm not an expert at voices but I could make out it was an eager voice. There was an air of expectancy in the air as my dad approached me.

"Dad, I will go to the monastery for one year but there are things I want in return."

"You name it" –was the eager reply. "Oh I'll give you a long list in a few days" – I said.

In truth there's nothing I wanted because I already had everything I wanted, but I said I'll give you a list just in case I would think of something and anyway it's not as if I was going to the monastery tomorrow there would be lots of time.

So I asked my dad when we intended to go to the monastery. (The monastery was located 40 kms away from Haridwar so we would have to catch a flight to Delhi and then there was a 4 hours drive from Delhi).

'We catch the flight tomorrow morning' my dad replied.

This shocked me out of my wits. "When did you make all the arrangements" I asked dad.

"Oh we spoke to the abbot Swami Sutradev 4 months back".

I went back to my room to digest these facts. My dad had already decided what I would do with my future. My marks were just a number, irrespective of my marks I would have landed up in the monastery. My dad had said he would give me total freedom in my decision regarding my future. I guess he didn't mean what he said or what he meant was I had total freedom to do whatever I wanted as long as it was what he wanted. There was no time to back out, I had already said yes. I had no idea what I should carry to the monastery. I had visited the monastery a few times but I had only entered the visiting areas of the monastery and I never stayed more than a few hours. These were purely social visits. I had to make these visits compulsorily to ensure I would get the money for vacations with friends. Dad was clear if I didn't go to the monastery I would not get funds from him to enjoy my vacation with friends.

Just then I heard my mom's voice, there was a broad smile on her face as she entered my room. She was proud of me I could tell.

"I'll just pack a few clothes for you and some essentials, everything else you need you will get at the monastery."

"Thanks mom" – I said.

I was 18 and my room was my own private den. I didn't appreciate anyone walking into my room but even then when it came to packing clothes, my mom always did my packing. In a way I felt she wanted to spend some time with me because she took an unusually long time to do the packing.

Neither mom nor grandpa would be coming along with me to leave me at the monastery and only my dad would be escorting me, - my mother informed me. After this she saw my moist eyes and broke down immediately.

'Oh it's just a year' – I consoled my mom and when my mother regained her composure she looked at me and said –"whatever happens you will do your best" and I said "mom I will do my best but I'm average, I'm not brilliant like dad or grandpa".

"Don't you worry about that, things will change that much I can assure you. I wouldn't part with you for one year if I was not dead sure it's for your good"-mom replied.

So with all my packing done I still had the entire day and night before I left for the monastery where I would be following rules and be disciplined. Freedom had never been worth more in my eyes. Suddenly I knew what it meant to be free. I immediately went towards the cage of my pet parrot Sulu and opened the cage door. I hoped Sulu would step out of the cage and soar towards the skies. Sulu did step out of the cage but after some time he walked back into the cage. May be freedom was

scary to Sulu, because he had grown used to captivity. May be it was because he was well looked after, so why bother to soar to the skies? There is nothing more mystical than a bird soaring in  the skies defying the laws of gravity which human beings are subject to. "Sulu I'm disappointed with you, take your freedom and go. Soar to the skies, it is your birth right" I said. But Sulu pretended not to understand what I was telling him. I pushed Sulu out of the cage and closed the cage door so that there was no way Sulu could get back into the cage. If Sulu chose to stay back in my room it was his choice but he would stay a free bird and definitely not in a cage.

And then I saw grandpa peek into my room. "Come in grandpa"– I said.

He looked at me and Sulu and smiled and said "That's exactly what we are trying to do to you. We are trying to help you break out of your cage. Your mind and body have taken over total control over the real you. You have to break out of the limitations created by your mind and body and realize who you truly are. You are not average or limited; you are like a bird in a cage. The mind and the body are the cage. Once you break out of the cage there is nothing you cannot achieve." I understood that I did not understand and I wanted badly to understand. My grandpa gave me a big hug and it felt good. I thought of informing my friends that I would be away for one year then I decided there was no point, I wouldn't know what to say and they wouldn't understand.

So it's funny, I had 1 day before I entered the monastery and I decided I would spend the day with myself. I closed

the door of my room and put on the music on full blast. But music had lost its charm and I was soon wondering as to what was the inner music monks listen to. My grandpa had told me when the mind and body are still you can listen to the inner music. He had also told me that the truth is only realized in silence. I knew my grandpa would not lie to me unless he had experienced something mystical.

I had a quiet dinner and then retired for the night. My mom had given me some sedatives so that I sleep well because there was a big day ahead, probably the most important day of my life.

I woke up early the next day and decided to take a walk in the garden outside my house. I had never really cared for flowers or the garden or actually nature in general. But today was different. I suddenly understood how beautiful flowers were and also why grandpa spent so much time in the garden listening to the birds chirping away early in the morning. You never really know what you've got until you've lost it. I looked at the watch and realized it was time to go.

I could hear my mom calling me. I had spent two hours in the garden, but it felt as if I've just come there. Time was flying away really fast. I suddenly understood what Einstein meant by relativity. I had mugged up the answer for my exams but I had never really understood. Today I understood.

$e=mc^2$
Albert Einstein

Very soon I was in the car on the way to the airport. My dad was silent and so was I. I guess there was not much to say. I was nervous but he could already see that in my body language. A father and son don't need words when they speak to each other. There is a communication which happens in silence because you are so close to each other.

My dad broke his silence once we were on the plane. He said, "I must give you a basic background of the monastery so that you are comfortable".

I just nodded in approval.

"This monastery was built 65 years back by Swami Jaidev who was the Guru of the present abbot Swami Sutradev. Swami Jaidev dropped his body about 30 years back and since then Swami Sutradev is the abbot of the monastery. Swami Sutradev had spend 18 years meditating in a cave in the Himalayas, after which he spent nine years in a forest near Haridwar where he used the time for his contemplation practices. This monastery is set up very close to the forest land near Haridwar where Swami Sutradev earlier resided. At some point of time these two sages met and Swami Jaidev invited Swami Sutradev into his monastery."

"So Swami Sutradev after 27 years of dedicated meditation in trying conditions just accepted Swami Jaidev as his Guru?" I asked. May be he wanted the comforts of a monastery was the thought that crossed my mind but I did not voice it to my dad.

"Well I believe he didn't just accept him just like that" – my dad replied.

"I believe they had a duel" dad added "Wow! A duel!" I got excited "what happened?" I asked.

"They both sat facing each other" and I believe they had a debate.

"What was the subject of the debate" – I asked.

"I believe it was the concept of God they debated on".

"What really happened there?" – I asked dad.

"Well I can't tell you exactly but Swami Sutradev took the position that God didn't exist and Swami Param Guru Jaidev took the position that God exists and everything that exists is for God's pleasure. Somewhere in the debate Swami Sutradev mentioned that he is neither the mind nor the body but the unqualified consciousness which is non dual. So then Param Guru Jaidev laughed and said you are just repeating the scriptures. Suddenly Swami Sutradev experienced something mystical. He experienced that the mind, body and consciousness are just very small gifts God has given us and he realized that God's gifts do not stop at consciousness. He realized that God's power is unlimited. He could gift someone the power to create universes like ours. So it's possible that our universe was created by a Power who had received his powers to create from God. Today you cannot understand anything beyond mind, body and consciousness because your understanding is limited. But you must understand it is your understanding which is limited and not that of God. Swami Sutradev immediately bowed down before Param Guru Jaidevji and immediately accepted him as his Guru. Swami Sutradev realized what he didn't achieve in 27 years of hard labour he had realized in an instant due to the grace of a master and it is important to have a good master and within a short time he picked up everything Param Guru Jaidev had to offer. So deep was his understanding that Param Gurudev declared him his successor several years before he dropped his body" – dad explained.

'Dad why do the monks all wear robes of different colours' – I asked.

'Oh! it's nothing much' – dad continued.

"Essentially the monks wear robes of 3 colours. White robes are worn by monks who are just starting out as monks or monk who renounce the world for a short period of time say one year. White is the symbol of purity. At this stage since they are just starting off they cannot understand everything and so they are trained to see things as good or bad, black or white etc. When their understanding matures and they are ready they are given yellow robes. They can now understand that colours are a higher truth. They can understand that a change in time, place and circumstances can change right and wrong or at least the perception of right and wrong. And the last category is the wearers of the orange robes. Orange is a sacred colour and the wearers of these robes are revered in the monastery. Of course several people in India wear orange robes and overnight declare themselves as Gurus so that they can have an easy life style but don't confuse them with the wearers of the orange robes in the monastery were my dad's instructions."

"So where will I be staying in the monastery" – I asked dad.

"Oh! The monastery is essentially divided into 3 parts. One part is the small school and dispensary which the monastery runs for the villagers. This part of the monastery is accessible to all. The second part of the monastery has housing facility for visitors, wearers of the white and yellow robes, it also has a library, a visiting room where the abbot meets visitors, a dining room for all, a recreation room which has a Table Tennis table, a sound proof meditation room, a lawn where the abbot meets all the residents for a question answer session everyday and a few retreat rooms. This is the part of the monastery you will be staying in. The third part of the monastery is where the abbot and the wearers of the orange robe reside. This was a forbidden and secret area of the monastery." My dad didn't know much about this part of the monastery as he had never visited this area in the monastery. This was a forbidden area where only the adepts were allowed.

I was already excited and smelt adventure. There's no way I would stay for a year in the monastery and not investigate this area of the monastery.

My dad looked at me and said – "You have that mischievous smile on your face"

I said nothing.

The plane was soon landing at Delhi airport and I knew the monastery was just a 4 hours drive now. I decided I would use the time to prepare my mind for the inevitable.

My dad tried to speak to me in the car but I replied in monosyllables and soon he was also silent.

We reached the monastery very late in the afternoon and on arrival we went straight to the reception area of the monastery where we were greeted by Swami Sunil. Swami Sunil was a white robe wearer who did the work of a manager in the monastery. He was efficient, well organized and within two minutes I had the keys to my room in which I would be staying for the next one year. I looked around and it was all quiet in the monastery, not a single soul moving around. May be the monks knew I was coming and decided to leave the monastery.

Then I heard Swami Sunil tell my dad – "All the monks are in the meditation chamber right now along with the abbot. In half an hour they will all come out and then you can meet the abbot. Please go to the room now and become comfortable".

My room was on the second floor of the monastery. The yellow robe wearers were on the ground floor. The white robe wearers were on the first floor. The second floor was reserved for visitors or temporary renounciates who in the eyes of the abbot were as good as visitors.

When I saw my room I was in a state of shock. It was just a room with a bed, a cupboard, a fan and an attached bathroom. I was used to air conditioning, cable TV, aesthetic wood work and the works. Any way I thanked God at least there was a decent bathroom. I unpacked my clothes in the cupboard and soon it was time to meet the abbot.

Dad and I stood outside the meditation chambers so that the abbot would see us when he exited the meditation chambers and call us for a private audience. The tradition was that the abbot would first exit the meditation chamber and only then would the others leave.

Soon enough I got a glimpse of the abbot Swami Sutradev. He was 92 years old but he walked with his back straight. Had I not known he was 92 years old I would not have believed. He was followed by Swami Ananddev who was the next in command at the monastery. I had met both Swami Sutradev and Swami Ananddev for a few minutes in my earlier compulsory visits to the monastery and had liked both of them. But I couldn't figure out whether they would be as cool if I was staying with them for an extended period of time.

The abbot saw us, smiled and with a wave of his hand beckoned us to come to the visiting room. I had been to this room in my earlier visits. It was a large well done up room where the abbot met visitors to the monastery. He had a smaller room but that was where he met the wearers of the white and yellow robes. The wearers of the orange robe met the abbot in the part off the monastery which was off limits to all except wearers of the orange robe.

There were only three wearers of the orange robe in the monastery i.e. the abbot Swami Sutradev, Swami Ananddev and Swami Bholanath. Swami Bholanath looked after the social outreach projects of the monastery and in my eyes was more of an administrator than a Swami, but I couldn't vouch for that because I was not sure. There were 13 wearers of the yellow robe and 21 official wearers of the white robe in the monastery.

My dad and I entered the visiting room and immediately both of us touched the abbots' feet as a mark of respect. The abbot asked us to sit and ordered a cup of tea for us.

"So is the young man ready for this experience" – the abbot asked.

"He is" – my dad replied.

"You want to stay here for one year of your own free will" – the abbot asked.

"Are we absolutely free or do we have only relative freedom in everything" – I asked choosing to answer his question with a counter question.

The abbot laughed, it was a long hearty laugh.

"Why did you laugh" – I asked the abbot.

"Well, I could either laugh or cry and I choose to laugh" – the abbot replied.

This statement was followed by another long hearty laugh.

At least he's in a good mood – I thought.

"So abbot Sir, what will be my schedule here for the next one year" – I asked.

"Well I could put you under Swami Ananddev or under Swami Bholanath" – the abbot replied.

Swami Ananddev looked after the meditation, Japa and contemplation routines at the monastery and Swami Bholanath looked after the social outreach projects.

"Since your grandpa and dad give large donations to the monastery regularly if I place you under Swami Bholanath I would be placing Bhola in a situation where there is conflict of interest, so I will place you under Swami Ananddev" – the abbot continued.

This was a very great relief to me; being placed under Swami Bholanath would have meant mopping the floor in the monastery or helping out in the kitchen or helping out in the school or dispensary. All the 21 white  robe wearers and the 13 yellow robe wearers were under Swami Bholanath and Swami Ananddev had no immediate responsibility of nurturing young disciples in the monastery. This was also so because Swami Ananddev who was 70 years old had been in complete silence for the last 24 years. Of course

 I was anxious because I would be having a master who was in complete silence. I could not figure out what his expectations would be from an 18 year old disciple. Swami Ananddev carried a pen and pad along with him everywhere, if you asked a question you would get a written reply on the spot.

"So you can see there is nothing to worry about and he will be very comfortable here".

The abbot subtly hinted, it was time for my dad to leave the monastery. My dad took the hint and got up to leave the room. I also got up, but the abbot said, "Where are you going, I'm not through with you" – after he said this he had a long and hearty laugh.

I went forward and touched my dad's feet. I know I could go through this ordeal only if he blesses me.

"Vijayi bhava" (be victorious) – My dad blessed me and left the room. I knew I would meet my dad only after one year. Physically I and my dad would be away for one year but I know his memories and his blessings were always mine.

"So where has your mind wondered off" – the abbot asked.

"No where sir" – I promptly replied.

"So who are you?" – the abbot asked.

Oops the old man has had a stroke of amnesia I thought.

"I'm Sudesh Kapoor" – I replied.

"Not your name" – "Who are you?" – the abbot asked.

I didn't understand. Probably the abbot has had a peculiar type of amnesia he knows but he doesn't know. So in order to evade the question I replied "I'm searching for myself", it was a safe and intelligent answer I thought.

"Are you lost somewhere, if you're not lost why would you need to search for yourself?" – the abbot asked.

Again the abbot had a long hearty laugh.

I felt really pissed off. This guy's having the time of his life at my expense. I mustered up the courage and asked him a question.

"Sir, who are you?"

The abbots' expression changed immediately, he become serious and spoke in a very serious tone.

"That would be my answer and the result of my search. I don't want my answer to influence your search. If I tell you, you will mug up my answer and repeat it parrot like to everyone else in the monastery. But I will give you a hint" the abbot continued "I am whatever He (God) would want me to be, a truth greater than that I cannot see".

"So sir, you don't believe in Karmas" – I asked.

"You are a smart lad" – the abbot replied.

"Karmas are useful but not everything my son. When time, place and circumstances change, perception of right and wrong changes" – the abbot continued.

"Karmas are the icing on the cake, very important and yet they can be irrelevant at times".

I was confused, I knew the monastery spent a lot of money, time and effort in running the school and dispensary for villagers and made huge efforts to make life comfortable for the villagers and here the abbot tells me Karmas are useful but not everything.

I requested the abbot – "Sir, I'm confused please elaborate".

"With pleasure" the abbot replied.

"You see, the universe spins on love and surrender to God, everything is for His pleasure. When you realize this you would have seen your original face".

"So Sir even if I do bad karmas but I pray to God no one can touch me" I asked the abbot. I was confident I had cornered the abbot. (My ego was starting to get swollen).

The abbot replied – "bad Karmas, what are bad Karmas?" "Bad in whose perception"? "Who has decided these karmas are bad?"

"Society has Sir!" I butted in.

"Unfortunately what society wants does not matter in the universe, only Gods' word counts" – the abbot replied.

"Sir, you cannot say this, you have to believe in Karmas, its there in all the scriptures". I was desperately trying to convince the abbot that his belief structure had to match that of everyone who preceded him.

"If I tell you there is a ghost sitting next to you would you believe?" – the abbot asked.

"Of course not" – I replied.

"If I said God was next to you, inside and outside everywhere, would you believe?" – the abbot asked.

"Of course!" – I replied.

"You do not believe in ghosts or other realms because you seek validation from your senses. If you do not see a ghost he does not exist but this rule does not apply to God even though you don't see God, you firmly believe He exists. The point is God is closest to you and you know He exists, you know it sub consciously" – The abbot continued.

"What's the point Sir?", "I'm confused" – I added.

"Everything in the universe is not as it may seem, you can have true perception of right and wrong only with the grace of God, keep an open mind" – The abbot replied and got up indicating that the meeting was at an end. He rang a small bell which he kept next to his bed.  Sudha, the abbots' personal assistant (who was a white robe wearer) came in and the abbot, instructed her to take me to Swami Anand dev's visiting room.

Soon I arrived at Swami Ananddev's visiting room and he was surprised to see me. I informed him that the abbot Swami Sutradev wanted me to be under him.

Swami Ananddev wrote something on his pad and handed it over to me.

"I don't take people under my wings because I am in complete silence" – the chit said.

I said – "I know Sir but the abbot wanted me to be under you."

I was trying to be as humble as I could but I was getting an eerie feeling this Swami was reading my thoughts.

"Do you mind if I test you" – Swami Ananddev wrote on a chit and handed it over to me.

Of course I minded but I said humbly – "No Sir, it's your prerogative"

"So Son, who are you?" he wrote on a chit and handed it over to me.

I saw the question and I smiled, I'll get full marks on this one – I thought.

I remembered the abbots' answer and I replied "I am whatever He (God) would want me to be, a truth greater than that I cannot see" I had given the abbots' answer word for word he couldn't flunk me on this one, I thought and beamed confidently.

I saw him scribbling away again on his pad and I thought he would be writing about how perceptive I am and that actually I didn't need to stay in the monastery for one year because I already know everything.

I saw the chit and I felt shattered. It said, "I was looking for a student not a parrot".

So in a rather humble tone I said "Gurudev Ananddev ji I really don't know all these big things, please guide me."

He was pleased and he started scribbling away again on his pad.

The chit said – "That's the first step, realizing you don't know and approaching a master".

"So Guruji seriously – who am I?" – I asked.

He scribbled on a chit, - 'You can go through lifetimes and never come close to the answer or you may crack the code in no time, either ways you will have a very comfortable life where all your needs are well looked after. God looks after his flock. Would you believe I have students in higher realms that are still searching?'

He has students in higher realms! I was sure all those years in silence had affected his mind but I didn't want to state my views. His wry smile made me feel he had read my thoughts.

I managed to summon up the courage and ask my tutor – "Gurudev is it possible to read others' thoughts?"

"Sometimes" – he replied scribbling away.

"When is it possible?" – I asked.

"When you do not cover your thoughts" – came the prompt reply. I was hoping the papers in his pad would not end otherwise he may terminate our meeting.

"How does our mind attract thoughts" – I asked and I saw him scribbling the answer on the pad.

"Thoughts come from seven zones, three believed to be good, three believed to be bad and the seventh zone is the zone of the sages, but don't worry about thoughts, there are realms higher than thoughts, an example is the realm of perception. The realm of perception is the land where the Gurus reside. Thoughts have no juice or control over you if you can detach yourself from your thoughts. But the highest realm is where you can have correct perception".

"Gurudev if you have students at higher realms, I wonder why they chose a Guru at a lower realm? I would want a Guru who is at a higher realm than me" I asked.

"Logical, but logic is a valid tool when all the infinite factors that exist in the universe are known. Logic is not a valid tool when there may be several factors unknown. I urge you to discard logic. It is nothing more than a trap of the mind" – the scribbled chit said.

"So Gurudev what is the plan for me"? I asked.

"If it takes life times of practice what will I achieve in one year?" I asked.

"Nothing" – He scribbled on the chit and handed it over to me.

I was visibly disappointed, why spend one year in a monastery if there was no benefit. I mustered up the courage and voiced my apprehensions.

"Life cannot be measured like a profit and loss statement. Sometimes to lose is to gain and to gain is to lose" – was the reply on the scribbled chit.

"Gurudev how do I measure my life?" – I asked.

"By what it is worth to others" was the reply on a scribbled chit.

This was very confusing, and I asked "so you are referring to my good Karmas".

"No, I'm talking about love!" – came the scribbled reply.

"By the way, Dumbo is your new name in the monastery! I don't speak and you don't understand we are a master and disciple made for each other" – was the scribbled reply.

This was interesting, Guru Ananddev was talking about love. It was an interesting topic for an 18 year old and I thought the Guru had caught my pulse. I thought I should find out the Guru's understanding about love.

"So Gurudev what is love?" – I asked.

"It is the reversal of our primary tendency i.e. the 'I' factor. It is because of love that man becomes fit for evolution, because he sees beyond his needs and his desires. It's not just an emotion; it is the vehicle for evolution" – came the scribbled reply.

"Our mind and body creates the illusion that all that we see around us is real but in the true sense love is the substance with which this illusion is spun. Love is the key for evolution" – the next chit said.

Meanwhile Gurudev was still scribbling away.

"The rules of the universe are laced with love. We have very short memories and this ensures that we forget the loved ones who have passed away and are no more with us. Our short memories are because of love. Sometimes to forget may be a very big blessing".

"We all know that we will die but are minds are configured in such a way that we don't think about death – this is an example of how the rules of the universe are laced with mother's love".

Clearly Gurudev's idea of love was different from mine.

"Gurudev Sir, do you accept me as your pupil" I asked.

"Yes – of course" – he replied via another chit.

"So what happens now?" – I asked the Guru.

"Well, I will give you a few precepts and initiate you" – was the scribbled reply.

"What precepts?" – I asked.

"I could give you the precept – never lie, but change in time, place and circumstances could warrant a situation where you should lie and speaking the truth would be wrong. Since you are Dumbo (a little dense). I will not give you any precepts to keep. See sometimes being a little dumb helps" – was Guru Ananddev's reply.

Had I not known about Guru Anandev's character, I would have sworn he really liked me and was doing some favouritism and making my life comfortable. From what I had heard, Guru Ananddev was a stickler for discipline, a very tough teacher. The yellow robe wearers who were allotted under him soon took a transfer and were allotted under Swami Bholanath who was a soft and considerate teacher. Under Swami Bholanath a disciple could pace himself as per his own capacity whereas Guru Ananddev often transferred far more than what a student could retain. He worked with his disciples as if there was no tomorrow and did not tolerate excuses which is why his disciples either took a transfer under Swami Bhola or ran away from the monastery.

"So Gurudev there are no precepts" – I asked.

"Yes none! Giving precepts to someone at your level would be dangerous, you do not understand much, please close your eyes" – came the scribbled reply.

I closed my eyes not bothering to question why.

"I have etched a mantra in your conscious, sub conscious and unconscious mind, do you know what it is" – the scribbled note said.

I just nodded I knew the mantra he had given me.

ॐ भूर्भुवः स्वः
तत्सवितुर्वरेण्यं
भर्गो देवस्य धीमहि ।
धियो यो नः प्रचोदयात् ।।

"You will practice this mantra all the time in your mind, it is perfectly etched in your conscious, sub conscious and unconscious mind so that you will never miss a word or mispronounce it even if you practice it at a very high speed" – the chit said.

"Gurudev, wouldn't this be cheating? I could practice this mantra very easily millions of times more than anyone else" – I asked.

Guru Ananddev looked at me smiled and soon scribbled the reply on a chit.

"This is not cheating, it is called the Guru's grace! The power was mine to give and I gave it to you. It is a gift to a disciple, don't bother about it".

I was excited, a mind to mind transmission of a mantra on the first meeting. The mantra was etched in my

conscious, sub conscious and unconscious mind so I could never mispronounce it or skip a word. Guru Ananddev was a Pandora's Box.

"What now Gurudev?" – I asked.

"As long as you practice the mantra regularly for the next one year, I don't really care; you're not bound by any of the monastery rules. You can make friends, enjoy yourself, and set your own schedule. You are a free man" – the scribbled chit said.

I was really pleased. Swamis are real cool people I thought.

"As long as you finish one million repetitions before you leave this monastery I don't really care. If you don't finish one million repetitions there will be penalties".

My views about Swami Ananddev swung to the other end of the pendulum very fast. Now I thought he was nothing less than a slave driver. To complete one million repetitions in one year I would have to put in 12 hours a day on the minimum. Where was the time to make friends, socialize, go to the library and read the scriptures etc?

"Of course the first 3000 repetitions are for the abbot, Bholanath and me so you will not get any benefits from those repetitions" – the chit said.

"Of course, I replied" I thought Guru Ananddev was very reasonable and had asked for a very small guru dakshina but Gurudev was still scribbling away.

"The benefits of the other repetitions will go in three equal parts to you, your family and the third part will go to people in need".

I looked at this chit from Guruji and said I was agreeable.

"Oh, so you will gift the abbot, Guru Bholanath and me the benefits of 3000 repetitions of the mantra? Do you think we are low down people who will accept a gift from you

and not give you anything in return?" – As I looked at the chit I smiled. I had read Guru Ananddev correctly; he had a very tough exterior and a very soft interior. He would take away from you only to find an excuse to give you more. I was excited at the prospects of gifts, if Guru Ananddev could very easily make a mind to mind transmission of a mantra there's no telling what the abbot and Guru Bholanath might give.

I know it doesn't look nice to ask the Guru straight to his face what the gifts were but I couldn't restrain myself and I blurted out.

"Gurudev, Sir what are the gifts?"

The mischievous smile on Gurudev's face told me he would not reveal the gifts to me right now. I would have to wait.

"It will be what you want and need, it will be revealed at an appropriate time" Gurudev had scribbled away.

I noticed that I didn't have much respect for Gurus before I entered the monastery but now I was beginning to really respect them.

Any way I was looking forward to meeting all the residents of the monastery. I thought Gurudev would now call one of the white robe wearers and introduce me.

"So Gurudev can I meet the others?" – I asked.

"No!" was the scribbled reply.

I was puzzled!

"You will stay in the forbidden part of the monastery where only orange bearers are allowed, which is of course only three of us. You can wear your jeans we won't mind" scribbled Gurudev.

This was absurd I had to stay in the monastery for one year and was not even given a white robe. What was worse was I would be totally cut off; food and other essentials would be provided to me when I required them but other than that I was on my own. I could decide when I would practice my mantra

and when I would read the scriptures, or I could just laze around and risk penalties at the end of one year. I had thought I would explore the forbidden part of the monastery and that it would be a big adventure. Now Gurudev put me up in the forbidden part of the monastery. I was sure there was nothing in the forbidden part of the monastery or they wouldn't have put me up there. They must have just forbidden people to enter that part of the monastery because the orange robe wearers may have wanted privacy. I would have a large space to myself and all the privacy in the world but I would not be interacting with anyone else.

I told Gurudev – "But I have already been allotted a room in the other part of the monastery and unpacked in that room".

Gurudev smiled – "No big deal, your belonging can be shifted" – the scribbled chit said.

"I have already passed on the instructions through telepathy, you are not at that level so I have to scribble on paper for you" – I looked at the chit and suddenly got cold feet. This monastery was soon getting to be a real weird place.

Isn't it weird they put up a total novice, a mere visitor for one year in an area where the white robe bearers and yellow robe bearers who have practiced for years are forbidden? Monks are eccentric people after all I gathered.

"Gurudev, why give me the honour of living in this area where even the yellow robe wearers are forbidden?" – I asked.

"We test people and have no pre-conceived notions, you did something right somewhere in this interview which forced me to upgrade your status and give you the privilege of living in a VIP area which is called the forbidden zone" – came Guruji's reply on a chit.

"Do you want to communicate through chits or do I now teach you telepathic contact?" – I looked at the chit and wondered how he would teach me telepathic contact. I wished to tell him I was very average and may not easily be able to learn telepathy.

"Bullshit"! – Was the masters reply.

There was no chit; I got the message transmitted to my mind, straight and direct.

Telepathy

I had established contact with my Gurudev.

Now we no longer needed chits to communicate. "It's all a gift! The moment you realize it, you will know there's nothing you have which makes you superior or inferior. As you get a glimpse of truth, the ego has no space to exist" – was the Master's message loud and clear.

"The universe spins on love and surrender to God! You should not doubt the abbots' word my child" – Gurudev reiterated.

"We have given you some gifts. We don't want you to show off before the white and yellow robe bearers. If you get the opportunity to show off, your ego will bloat and you will see nothing beyond yourself. And the whole purpose of this stay at the monastery will be lost."

I agreed with Gurudev and said "It will be as you so desire". I realized there was no need to speak; Gurudev had already received my thoughts.

Guruji Ananddev waived his hand and the meeting was now over. I got up and left the room.

I asked my Guru telepathically which was the room I should go to.

I got a sharp lashing reply telepathically, "Demonstrations are over, I have a vow of silence but you don't. Use your mouth. Are you trying to show off before me?"

I decided I would never try to use telepathy again.

My new room in the forbidden part of the monastery was very comfortable. I had all the facilities of a home. I had a fridge, TV, plush furniture, a stereo system and everything I had hoped for. The ambience in the bath room was even better than home. This is not going to be as bad as I thought. I  had a target of mantra repetitions and as long as I met my target the orange robe wearers didn't care what I did with my time.

I didn't know how the year would pass after all I was cut off from everybody except the three orange robe wearers who would be my mentors and guardians for the period.

I tried to figure out what I did right but couldn't. I got a prompt telepathic message from Guru Ananddevji.

'Love will meet love,

Manipulation will meet manipulation'

Nuts! I said. He can use telepathy with me and I am forbidden to use it with him.

'Rules are rules' was the prompt reply. I guess I was pretty tired hence I decided to call it a day.

"Everything I have to teach you I will teach in the next few days after that you just have to practice" – I got Guruji's message loud and clear.

I was pretty tired and had a headache from all the telepathy business but Gurudev was not in a mood to give me a break.

"It's time to tell you what my gift is. Nothing will distract you from your goal of one million repetitions. So in short I'm assuring you of success in your assignment but what the abbot and Guru Bhola have given you only they can reveal. It's between you and them".

                                                    The Perceptionist

I thought if Gurudev's telepathic messages continued I would have a bad headache. But there's nothing I could do, I had no control over my mind.

"That's temporary" Gurudev replied, "You have no idea of the potency of the mantra I have given you. Many receive this mantra, few practice it. Of those who practice it there are none who are known".

Nuts – I thought so there's no scope for fame now that I'm practicing this mantra. So why practice this mantra?

"It's a purifier, unless you purify your mind I cannot take you to higher practices" – was the telepathic reply.

That makes sense I thought.

"When your mind is purified you don't need the senses to see, you will see through your inner eyes" came Gurudev's telepathic message.

And I remembered both grandpa and dad had spoken about seeing through inner eyes. If I practice I may be onto something big I thought. I then thought I had been given a mantra and the guru had assured the successful completion of my assignments, isn't this cheating?

"It's mine to give"– was my Guru's response.

"You will get fame but be unaware about it" was the telepathic message from the abbot. This was the abbots' gift. I couldn't figure out of what use fame was if you were not aware about it but I knew the abbot would gift me either what I wanted or what I needed.

The Background....

This set my mind wondering about what Swami Bholanath, the most compassionate Guru would give me.

"Nothing"- was the prompt telepathic reply from Bholaji. I felt bad may be he wasn't such a big Swami after all – he would gift me nothing.

 "One day you will understand – nothing" was the next message from Swami Bholaji.

I realized he was just playing with me; after all I was just like his grandchild. I didn't feel guilty anymore even though I was angling for a gift from Bholaji so what? Children love gifts. I was sure he was hiding the gift from me till the last moment.

"You will effortlessly communicate with all the three orange robe bearers" is my gift.

I felt I would never fully comprehend the enormity of this gift. It was like having three guardians or protectors and that felt good. "Sacred protectors is the word" came Guru Ananddev's telepathic reply.

"We will never be with you but we will always be communicating with you" Guru Ananddev reassured me.

You can rest now all that you should know has been told to you. I guess there was nothing more to do but to sleep peacefully and try to set up a schedule of practice for the next day.

The next few days I spent practicing the mantra that was given to me. I didn't want to disappoint my Gurus. Also I didn't want to wander around much as I was living in the forbidden part of the monastery.

A few days later.......

I heard Swami Bholanathji voice calling and I immediately went out of my room to meet him.

"So do you want to look around" – he asked.

"But Sir, this is the forbidden part of the monastery" – I replied.

"Oh! You won't be moving around alone, I will be with you giving you a tour of this part of the monastery".

I got excited and immediately said "Yes! Of course I would like to look around".

Immediately I followed Swami Bholanathji, he told me that this part of the monastery had 10 secret chambers.

The first chamber was the chamber which maintained several old secret manuscripts. The manuscripts if used by an adept could give very lucid details about ones past lives. I wanted to enter this chamber but Swami Bholanathji said no. He said.

"Nature has created a block for a very good reason".

I asked "Of what use is this chamber if people could not enter?"

"We use this chamber to know about past lives of those who wish to enter this monastery as robe bearers, so that we can give them appropriate training. So you see we use this chamber for good purposes only" – he replied.

We were close to the second chamber and Swami Bholanathji explained that this chamber had manuscripts that helped in accurately predicting future outcomes. Again I was not allowed to enter this chamber. This chamber was used by the monks only for the welfare of the pupils. If a big disaster was to fall upon any of the pupils the masters would try to soften the blow. They would not interfere with the outcomes but they would try to get the pupil ready mentally to withstand the blow.

The third chamber was the chamber of mirrors. In this chamber a pupil sees himself as he is. This chamber is used by the masters to keep their own ego under check.

"Would you like to enter this chamber?" – Swami Bholanathji asked me.

"No, thank you Sir for the offer" – I politely replied, you never know what I might see there I thought. Not seeing is safer.

"May be another time" – Swami Bholanathji replied.

"What about the other seven secret chambers?" I asked.

"You will be told about them only when you have had the courage to enter the chamber of mirrors and see yourself as you really are" – he replied indicating that my tour of the forbidden part of the monastery was at an end.

I really wanted to know what was there in the other seven chambers but I didn't want to enter the chamber of mirrors and see who I was.

"Any way to know about the other seven chambers you have to get the permission of the Yakshas and pro Yakshas who are the protectors of those seven chambers" – he continued.

"Who are these Yakshas and pro Yakshas" – I asked him.

"Yakshas are a tribe who are dedicated to their search for God. They have irradiated fear and pain. Even after millions of years of effort their search continues" – Gurudev said.

"Millions of years? Impossible!"

"Oh I forget to tell you – they don't die, but they can't have children either" Gurudev added.

"And the pro-Yakshas" – I asked.

"Oh! They are female Yakshas!" – Gurudev added.

"So they live forever, but can't have children" – I asked.

"You've got the point, and only those they adopt as their children can go to the last seven chambers" – Gurudev added.

"So how do they adopt you as a child? – I asked Gurudev.

"Well you have to fight a duel" – Gurudev replied.

"Oh! That's gross! How horrible!" – I replied.

"No you don't understand! It's a debate and the topic is known to all the robe wearers in the monastery" Gurudev replied.

"What's the topic?" – I asked curiously.

"Concept of God" – Gurudev replied.

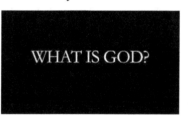
WHAT IS GOD?

"You don't have to win the duel, all you have to do is win some respect" – Gurudev added.

"Oh, I was good in debates you know" – I told Gurudev.

Gurudev just smiled. I thought he would tell me there are white robe wearers and yellow robe wearers who have not had the guts to fight a duel and here I wanted to take a chance. All I had to do was go into the chambers of mirrors, see myself in the mirror and then fight a dual with the Yakshas. How bad could it be after all, I saw myself in the mirror every day. But something told me it was obviously not easy or everyone else would have tried.

Gurudev escorted me back to my room and instructed me to carry on with my mantra, months passed and I kept pursuing my mantra to no avail. I had built up a good working schedule.

The Background....

I would wake up at 3 a.m. in the morning and start practicing my mantra. Of course I don't take full credit for this, if I didn't start practicing by 3.15 a.m. my Guru woke me up with a sharp tongue lashing telepathically. The usual message was "lazy bones, rise and shine". So it was difficult in the first few days but after the 1st month I never needed to be woken up because I had formed the habit of waking up by 3 a.m. and starting my japa. My mind was never steady on the japa and after sometime would wander off but I had a daily target of japa and could not let it wander off for long. If I took a long break of over 15 minutes from my japa my Guru would gently remind me my life in the monastery had a purpose. Sometimes I wondered whether mechanically doing the japa would have any benefit but my Guru assured "It's the effort that counts".

Even though I knew the mantra was not working for me I kept going on, until the day one year elapsed.

I was escorted by Guru Ananddev and Guru Bholanath to the abbot's chamber. I touched the abbot's feet and the abbot said, "you have done well; you have dedicatedly pursued the mantra for one year. Your parents and grandpa are waiting anxiously to pick you up".

I was dejected.

"Sir, I have spent one year in the monastery but there's nothing I have learnt. I was average when I walked in and when I am walking out I am still average" – I told the abbot.

The abbot had a long hearty laugh.

"Average is a relative word and a matter of perception" – the abbot said.

"Over a period of time the mantra will start its work in your mind if you practice it regularly. Then you will see the difference" – the abbot added.

"Pack up your luggage and go to the second part of the monastery where your parents are waiting. All the formalities have been done. You can leave immediately," – the abbot added.

I said my good byes to all the three gurus and packed my bags and went to the room in which my parents and grandpa were waiting for me. I hugged my parents and grandpa. They were really happy to see me again. On the drive back to the airport I felt as if I was coming alive again after spending one year in seclusion. The flight back home was uneventful.

So now I was a XII grade pass with 69% who had spent one year in a monastery. The problems of life still remained. What I would do in the future with my life was still a mystery. I knew after I reached home this subject would come up. It didn't matter anymore.

When we reached home I was feeling pretty tired so I decided to go to my room and take a nap. When I woke up after a few hours I felt I knew what I wanted to do in life. I would do anything that was creative. I decided I wanted to be an apprentice at an Ad agency. I was sure marks were just a number and  creative people don't bother about marks. So I went to my dad and told him what I wanted to be and he said "It's your life – go for it."

Only when you don't fear failure, life opens the doors of success.

– was the telepathic message from my Guru Anand dev.

Back at home.....

I had a month's free time before college started (I would be completing my B.Com) and I decided I would spend the time constructively. I wanted to ultimately work in an ad agency and I figured that the best way to be successful in an ad agency was to have knowledge of varied fields which may seem unconnected. I knew now everything was not as it may seem and there was nothing which was unconnected in the universe. After all Steve Jobs the founder of Apple Inc took classes in calligraphy and used this knowledge when he built the computer. It is his knowledge of calligraphy which ensured that the Mac had multiple typefaces and proportionally spaced fonts. And who can forget that the double entry system of book keeping (which is the pride of every accountant) was invented by a monk so that he could keep proper records of the accounts of the monastery. Luca Pacioli (a monk in the Franciscan order) invented the system of book keeping when he was asked to keep records of the finances of the monastery.

So, I decided that I would take classes on astronomy in my vacation time of one month. I decided I would rope in my friend Ramesh to take the classes along with me. My parents were a bit shocked that I would want to join classes in astronomy when my ambition was to work in an ad agency but my parents had an open mind. They understood that my mind was opening up to possibilities and that I had an urge to push the boundaries and explore the universe around me. My friend Ramesh who had got 86% and had got admission in science with great difficulty was not enthusiastic (he was now one year senior to me) but his parents were very enthusiastic. Ramesh's dad thought it was a brilliant idea and so Ramesh had no option but to take classes on astronomy along with me. I could not understand why Ramesh was not enthusiastic, after all this was his field. But soon I realized I was thinking differently, I wanted to know more about everything. I was curious about the universe, about man's nature, about life and death and about love. I was not under any pressure to learn, in fact learning and co relating things was becoming a pleasure.

On our first day in the astronomy class Ramesh carried a lot of books to the class, I carried no books as I had decided I would go with an open mind and a clean slate. Our astronomy teacher, Mr. Pradeep Kumar was an old man of around 62 years but he looked much older. You could make out that he enjoyed teaching new students because he could show off his knowledge and his students were usually spell bound.

The first question he asked us in the class was 'what is the centre of the universe?' No one raised his hand to reply. I decided I would take a chance and raised my hand. Mr. Pradeep Kumar was pleased and asked me to answer.

"Sir, if we believe that ours is an infinite universe, then any star or planet can be the centre of the universe. Because any star your choose still would have infinite space on all sides".

Our Sir was not pleased.

"There is no centre of the universe. Ours is an expanding universe. Take a balloon and fill air in it, the more air you fill the more the balloon expands. The surface of the balloon is like the space in the universe." Of course I didn't understand.

I could not figure out how the space of the universe could be compared with the space of a balloon. Somehow I figured out that physicist's ignored dimensions and wanted everything in black and white in perfect formulas. Everything had to be perfectly calculable for all time. Time, place and circumstances may change but the formulas had to be perfect for all time. There could be no variation. It was a search for perfection. I felt perfection was a waste of time. Life is measured by what it is worth

to others, my Guru had taught me. The real measure of life is lost if you live reliant on numbers. Mathematics had taught me that one minus one is zero. So if I have one rupee and I decide to give it away I am left with zero rupees i.e. nothing. Surprisingly it is this 'nothing' which has fascinated mystics. I too was fascinated by 'nothing'. After all it had been a matter of serious research by philosophers. Parmenides (5th Century BC) had argued that "nothing" cannot exist. Achieving "nothingness" as a state of mind in Buddhism and Hinduism allows one to be focused on an activity at a level of intensity such that the results achieved, could not be achieved by conscious thinking.

"So can you give us the answer" – I heard Sir's voice.

"What" – I replied.

"Where were you? I am asking you the speed at which you have to go if you have to go from A to B in one hour."

Sir had given a problem to the class and instead of working on the problem my mind was roaming around.

I had to think fast.

"Sir, I have a basic question" – I replied.

"Yes! Please ask" – Sir replied.

"Sir, space is three dimensional and time is one dimensional, can we accurately divide them and get speed?"

"Stupid questions will not be entertained please concentrate on the problem at hand" – was Sir's reply.

I realized Sir didn't have an open mind. He had a lot of knowledge and probably was a master at his field but he was not open to visualizing things differently. Perhaps the universe was not so much a mystery to him as it was to me. I know that I knew nothing and Sir had decided as far as physics was concerned he knew everything. Having an open mind was very important, my Guru had taught me. Here I could see even my elders could not manage to have an open mind. I remembered my Guru's words and his technique of having an open mind.

"Everything you believe to be true, believe that the opposite is also true and the world will open up enormous possibilities for you" – my Guru had said.

The sages had no firm concepts and believed in flowing like water. Everything is possible if you step out of the cage of the mind. It is the mind which limits your options and tells you nothing is possible when in truth we live in a universe where anything is possible.

"Sudesh, have you dozed off?" I heard Ramesh's voice and my mind came back to the classroom and I became conscious of things around me.

"No, yaar I'm awake" – I replied.

"The first lesson is over, it's time to go home" – he said.

Ramesh and I left the classroom and we made our way to my car. I dropped Ramesh at his house and then I went home.

"How was your class?" Dad asked when I reached home.

"Not as exciting as I thought it would be" – I replied.

I couldn't tell my Dad I had joined the class to explore the mysteries of the universe. At least that's what I thought would happen in the class. What actually happened was that we were given a bunch of formulas to mug up and several problems to solve as home work. This was not my definition of education.

Motion with constant acceleration: main equations

$$V_x = V_{0x} + a_x t$$

$$x = x_0 + V_{0x} t + \frac{1}{2} a_x t^2$$

$$V_x^2 - V_{0x}^2 = 2a_x (x - x_0)$$

I went back to my room and sat wondering

what astrologers would think about our astronomy teacher's rigid news. Astrologers believe that relative positions of celestial bodies are signs of or causes of destiny, personality, human affairs and natural events. Some astrologers believe that the planets control fate directly; others believe that they determine personalities. I was now curious about astrology. After all nothing in the universe is unconnected. I thought enough of astronomy, now I will read up on astrology. Although astrology cannot be classified as a science because it lacks empirical support, supplies no hypotheses, and resolves to describe natural events in terms of scientifically untestable super natural causes, I was interested in it.

Is there any truth in astrology I wondered? If astrology is possible, then where lay free will?

I had visited the second chamber in the monastery where the orange robe bearers used manuscripts to predict future outcomes. They never interfered with outcomes my Guru had told me. If a big disaster was to fall upon any of the pupils the masters would try to soften the blow. The effort was to try to get the pupil mentally ready to withstand the blow.

The core beliefs of astrology were prevalent in parts of the ancient world and are epitomized in the Hermetic maxim, "as above, so below". Tycho Brahe used a similar phrase to summarize his studies in astrology.

"By looking up I see downward"

So does the movement of planets really affect our future or behaviour? One thing was for sure the tides on the earth are mostly generated by the gradient in intensity of the moon's gravitational pull from one side of the earth to the other.

I didn't know whether everything is pre determined or we have free will but one thing was for certain to explore astrology I should understand mathematics. Everything centred on calculations. No wonder practical mathematics has been a human activity for as far back as written records exists. Mathematicians seek out patterns and formulate new conjectures. Albert Einstein had said that "as far as the laws of mathematics refer to reality, they are not certain, and as far as they are certain, they do not refer to reality". Suddenly I was interested in mathematics. I wanted to know why, I wanted to know how, and I wanted to ask why not? Numbers were suddenly very interesting. After all the binary numeral system used two symbols, O and 1 and is used internally by all modern computers. With two options O and 1 or Yes and No, man has built such sophisticated equipment. What to say about the Creator, who has built the human mind which has infinite possibilities. A computer is slave to logic and programming. We are not slave to logic and have the capability to go beyond logic and also the capability to override our own programming. Hence the scope for love, courage, chivalry etc. I was dismissive of logic because my Guru had told me 'Logic is a valid tool only if, the infinite factors in the universe are known' but he had also told me 'examine the truth with no prejudice'. So

I decided in the morning I would ask my Grandpa what logic was.

My grandpa was a famous writer. I idolized my grandpa and knew he would enlighten me.

Early the next day morning I met grandpa at the breakfast table and asked him –

"Grandpa, what is logic"?

"Why the sudden interest in logic" – grandpa asked.

"Oh I'm suddenly interested in everything" – I replied.

The Chinese logical philosopher Gongsun Long (ca 325 – 250 BC) proposed the paradox. "One and one cannot become two, since neither becomes two" – grandpa replied.

"What are you trying to say grandpa?"

"Correct perception of facts is important for you to arrive at correct solutions" – grandpa replied.

"If your perception is correct, logic is irrelevant, because you will arrive at the correct decision" – grandpa continued.

"Logic is the formal science of using reason. But how will you use logic, after all you have dreams of joining an ad agency after college. Concentrate and focus on your dream"– grandpa said.

"Oh grandpa, knowledge never goes waste" – I replied.

"I'm sure the buying patterns of people are logical, all I have to do is research the patterns and establish why? Once I have spotted the pattern and established its logic, I'm sure I'll do wonders in the ad agency" – I replied.

"You've become pretty smart" – grandpa replied.

I felt puffed up. Praise from my grandpa meant the world to me.

"Not only that, grandpa after using the mantra in the monastery for over a year, I realized that the orange robe bearers had used psychology on me.

"How's that" – grandpa asked me.

"Well before I started, Gurudev told me that I had his blessings and that I would successfully complete the repetition of the mantra one million times in one year. After this I was dead sure I would succeed. I realize now all Gurudev did was to wake me up a couple of times when I overslept. He did not interfere in any way. I was so sure I would succeed that I put in far more effort than I normally would. This was a very powerful use of psychology by Gurudev".

Grandpa smiled at me.

No wonder grandpa reveres Gurudev – I thought.

I was impressed and also wonder struck by the power of psychology. No wonder psychology literally means "study of the soul". If only I could understand psychology. Psychology is the science of behaviour and mental processes, if you understand psychology you will understand how people and groups will behave. If the ad agency won't have me because I'm not creative enough, I'll do wonders in the stock market I thought.

I spend the rest of the day thinking about the power of psychology. Gurudev had given me his blessing and told me that I would be successful. Because I had so much faith in him and I believed in him there was no doubt in my mind that I would succeed. And I succeeded. Psychology was definitely worth exploring I thought. If I understood myself and I understood how and why I behaved in a particular manner I could extrapolate how others would behave. I had seen a very powerful demonstration at the monastery. Gurudev had used my mental conditioning and belief system to guide my future behaviour in a particular manner. It is like striking the opponent without moving a muscle, which is the goal of every martial artist.

I put on the music and decided to relax for some time. Then I saw grandpa entering my room.

"Why wait until you graduate, you can be an apprentice at an ad agency along with college" – grandpa told me.

"Why not, I'm game" I replied.

My commerce college was only three hours in the morning, so I had a lot of free time.

My grandpa had been a famous writer and had a lot of friends in ad agencies so getting me hired as an apprentice was not a big deal. I decided to do a little bit of research before I landed up for the interview.

The ad agency (Rocking kills) I walked into for my interview was a large agency. They were into a range of products. I figured this would be good because I would get varied experience. So I walked in for the interview with a one page bio data. I was a 19 year old who had spent the last one year in a monastery. And to make matters worse I had 69% in my XII grade exams and I was looking for a part time apprenticeship after my college hours.

I had expected the atmosphere to be absolutely informal. I thought people would be walking around in their shorts with spiked hair and tattoos. Surprising this was not so. People were fully dressed and pretty formal. And my boss to be, Mr. Sujay Sathe kept me waiting for over an hour. His secretary was very polite about it and kept replying "Just 10 minutes" every time I asked her "How long more it would take?"

Finally Mr. Sujay Sathe called me in. He asked for my resume which I confidently handed over to him.

"Just 69% in your XII grade" – Mr. Sujay asked.

"Yes Sir" – I politely replied.

"Why should we take you" – he asked.

"I'm hard working and diligent" – I replied.

"Everybody is, so what's new" he asked.

"As you can see I have spent one year in a monastery. My perspective is different. I will surprise you with my insights" – I replied.

"OK this is my blazer. Its rubbish, I throw it in the dustbin. It reminds me of my wife because she bought it for me. Sell me this blazer and we'll hire you" – Mr. Sujay said.

I was in a tight spot knowing Mr. Sujay's mood, there was no way he would buy this blazer from me. I thought maybe it was just an excuse to pack me off. I could understand that if I presented the good qualities of the blazer it may not have any impact. If I explained to boss why he needed the blazer, this might not impress him as every aspiring apprentice would have tried this strategy.

"Sir is it important that I sell this blazer or do I have to sell the blazer to you only" – I asked.

"Come again" – he replied.

"If you hire me to sell soap, will you be interested in the number of soaps I sell or will you be focused on the fact that I should sell soaps to a particular market only' – I asked.

"I'm interested in sales – I don't care who you sell to" he replied.

"So Sir, can I find a new market for your blazer. If you give me your wife's number I'm sure I could convince your wife this blazer is not rubbish" – I replied.

He burst out laughing – Yes, why limit yourself to one market. When the market is saturated create a new market. Do you have any other strategy?

"Of course I do" I replied.

"What's that?" he asked.

"I was planning to sell you a specially designed dustbin in which you could throw jackets and blazers which you believe are rubbish" – I replied.

strat·e·gy
(strãt' ə-jē) n.
1. Plan of action designed to achieve a particular goal.

"So now you are selling me a new product?" He asked.

"Yes Sir, it's the latest. Specially designed dustbins for throwing jackets" – I replied.

"What are you doing" – he asked.

"Creating a new product to meet your new requirements, Sir" – I replied.

"Where does this go?" – He asked. "Assuming I buy your specially designed dustbin."

"Sir, then you have a specially designed dustbin with no jacket to throw in it. Might I suggest you buy this jacket so that you have something to throw in that expensive dustbin you just bought" – I replied.

"What are you trying to do?" he asked.

"Reverse pull" I replied.

"Creating the circumstances so that you feel there is a need for the product" – I continued.

He looked at me and smiled.

"If it were only up to me I would take you, let's see what boss feels' – Mr. Sujay said "boss is normally against hiring teenagers" – he added he picked up the intercom and spoke to his boss Mr. Ajit Saraf and briefed him.

He then picked up the intercom and called his secretary Shirin and asked her to escort me to Mr. Ajit Saraf's cabin.

I followed Shirin to Mr. Saraf's cabin. Shirin was everything a secretary should be, pretty, graceful and efficient. I was sure working with Shirin was going to be a

The Perceptionist

pleasure. I was quite sure Shirin and I would be on the same wavelength.

When I reach Mr. Ajit Saraf's cabin Shirin introduced me to his secretary Gracy. She was far older than Shirin and I figured she was in her forties. But she was very efficient and within two minutes I was entering Mr. Ajit Saraf's cabin.

I don't know where my mind was, I never saw the rug in front of me and I tripped and fell.

"Are you all right" – Mr. Saraf asked me. His voice exhibited concern I picked myself up quickly and replied "Thank God I've fallen into good company".

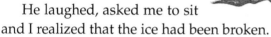

He laughed, asked me to sit and I realized that the ice had been broken.

"Will you have tea or coffee?" – He asked "tea" – I replied.

He picked up the intercom and ordered tea for both of us.

"So what did you learn in the monastery?" – Mr. Saraf asked me.

"Well nothing much – just a few mantras" – I replied.

"Well so was the trip a waste of time?" – He asked.

"No, not really" – I replied.

"I perceive things differently now" – I added.

"Please elaborate" – he said.

"Sir, the monks believe in expanding their horizons" – I replied.

"How can you apply all that you learnt there to the real world? This is the real world. There's no room here for losers. Does what you learnt at the monastery have any real value here, in the real world" – he asked.

I was sure Mr. Saraf was going to be a hard nut to crack. He was definitely not impressed with my monastic education. He broke the silence by asking me.

"So what is advertising all about?"

"Sir, it's all about communication. I have to get the message across in the shortest possible time". I replied.

"So tell me what you learnt in one year at the monastery" – he asked.

"Faith and perseverance is what I learned" – I replied.

"Both useless in the real world" – Mr. Saraf replied.

"Impress me!" Mr. Saraf added.

He looked around the room and said "sell me something I don't need".

"I'm a non smoker, try to sell me a cigarette" – he added.

I myself was a non smoker although a few of my friends smoked.

"I'll try sir" – I replied.

"Good" – he said.

He picked up a pen and handed it over to me and said "Assume this is a cigarette and sell it to me."

"Well, you don't have to smoke the cigarette" I picked up the pen and said.

"It's a new cigarette – you just hold it in your hand for style" – I said.

"Its stylish to have a cigarette in your hand and you don't have to smoke it so there are no health issues" – I added.

The Perceptionist

"So what are you trying to do" – he asked.

"Introducing a new product, Sir" – I replied.

"It's a very expensive cigarette which you just hold in your hand for style. You don't actually smoke this cigarette. It's for non smokers" – I added.

"What?" he asked.

"You see sir the world is divided into two parts, smokers and non smokers. I'm trying to erase this division. Now there will be cigarettes for smokers and cigarettes for non smokers" I added.

"Would you buy such a cigarette" – I asked.

"May be" he replied.

"I'm not interested in new markets or new products you sell me this cigarette" – Mr. Saraf said pointing to the pen.

"Sell a cigarette to a non smoker" – I asked.

"Yes – if you can I'll hire you, not as an apprentice but two levels higher" he replied.

Mr. Saraf had thrown a challenge and I had no option but to accept, I felt my dreams of working in 'Rocking Kills' depended on my performance in the next few minutes.

"But Sir, can you answer a few questions" – I asked.

"Go ahead ask" – he replied.

"You have never smoked?" I asked.

"Never, I'm dead against smoking" – he replied.

"Well?" he asked.

"Sir, one thing I learnt at the monastery, mental conditioning is most difficult to reverse."

"So" he asked.

"I can't work miracles" I replied.

"But if you give me the opportunity I will do excellent research. All the decision you will take will be based on facts and figures."

"So, you're dumping intuition" – he asked.

"No Sir, intuition will also show me the way forward" I replied.

"So, young lad – you fail" –Mr. Saraf's replied.

"May be destiny has something better in store for me" – I replied sadly.

"So you attribute failure to destiny and success to your own efforts" he asked.

"No Sir" – I replied.

Just then Mr. Saraf received a call from his boss Mr. Ajay Singh. I could make out whatever it was it was good news because Mr. Saraf couldn't stop laughing away.

Mr. Saraf's mood had changed completely.

"Rocking kills, has just added a very big client. We are not geared up to meet the client's requirements. We need to hire a lot of people" Mr. Saraf said excitedly.

Then he looked at me and extending his hand forward said.

"You're hired".

I was completely taken by surprise. Here Mr. Saraf had failed me and a few seconds later one phone call changed everything. Clearly I was at the right place at the right time.

"Thank you Sir" – I replied.

He looked at me and said again "you're hired".

I smiled and again said – "Thank you sir".

Your marks are average but there's something you have that's not definable. You have presence of mind and a knack for searching out solutions.

He was now praising me when a few minutes back he was sending me home.

"Thank you sir" – I said once again.

I could not tell him but I knew what I had, the monks call it awareness. I am limited but my father is not.

And as Jesus had said 'I and my father are one'.

"And in complete silence and stillness you can hear the sound of the one hand clapping" came my Gurudev's telepathic message.

I went back to my car; I felt I was floating in the air. My driver Jai Singh looked at me and asked.

"Sir, how was the interview"

"I got the apprenticeship at 'Rocking Kills'"

"That's very good Sir" – Jai replied.

"Rocking Kills is the best ad agency" – I added.

"Yes Sir" – my driver Jai replied.

"Where to sir?" – my driver asked.

"Home" I replied.

I reached home and told my parents I had got the apprenticeship. I felt pretty proud. I didn't know whether I had got the apprenticeship because Grandpa had put in a word or whether I had got it on my merits or it was plain luck. But I knew I had got an entry and now it was up to me to work hard and excel.

"You've made it into 'Rocking Kills'?" – grandpa asked.

"You bet, of course!" – I answered.

"And it's thanks to you and the blessings of the three sages who have always guided me".

"Our blessings are always with you" – grandpa replied.

The Background....

"What now?" – grandpa asked.

"Where are the celebrations?" – grandpa asked.

We decided we would go out to the Oberoi and have a celebratory dinner. While we were having dinner I asked dad and grandpa.

"How would you sell a cigarette to a non smoker?"

"Well it depends on his conditioning" – grandpa said.

"If he is rigidly opposed to smoking you don't have a chance but if he has an open mind you have a chance. If his mind is impressionable you have a chance. If the climate is cold you have a very good chance".

"So what would you have done in my place" – I asked dad.

"I wouldn't have got selected" – grandpa told me.

I felt puffed up. I had not told grandpa or my parents that Mr. Saraf had actually failed me and was in most probabilities going to send me home until he received a phone call from his boss. That phone call changed everything. I was in the right place at the right time. Was it destiny? Was it Karmas? Or was it just a gift from the sages?

I was pondering over the questions for a long time.

Is there free will or is there something like destiny?

"When you believe you have no choice, know for certain you do have choices" – came Guru Anand Dev's telepathic reply.

"What you want is unimportant,

there is no end to wants,

choose your wants appropriately"

– Was Guru Bholanath's telepathic message.

"This moment will not come again,

treasure it, cherish it and always wonder destiny or free will"

– Was the abbot's telepathic message.

 The Perceptionist

The abbot stops over....

After just two days of celebrating my selection as an apprentice at 'Rocking Kills' dad informed me that the abbot was returning from his overseas trip. The abbot would be stopping in Mumbai for a few hours. My dad asked me whether I would like to accompany him to meet the abbot. I said – "I will be delighted to accompany you".

So both dad and I got into the car and told Jai (our driver) to take us to the airport. We reached early and had to wait for almost an hour for the abbot to come out of the airport. There was a white robe bearer Shiva who took care of the abbot's luggage. Soon Shiva and the abbot were with us in the car and we were headed home. The abbot had many food restrictions, so mom had been quite busy since early morning making sure our cook was preparing the food as per the instructions provided by Swami Veer, who was the head cook at the monastery.

On reaching home, I insisted that the abbot visit my room for some time. The abbot agreed. Once I was seated alone with the abbot in my room I told the abbot,

"Gurudev I got selected as an apprentice at Rocking Kills. That's a very big Ad agency. I will be doing a lot of creative work. It's just what I always wanted".

The abbot smiled and asked.

"So you passed the interview."

"Yes" – I replied.

The abbot nodded and asked again.

"Did you pass or did fate intervene?"

I looked at the abbot and said.

"Actually Sir, I was almost rejected. Then the agency got a large order. I was at the right place at the right time".

"What are your interests" – the abbot asked.

"I like to research facts" – I replied and the abbot asked me to go on.

"I've developed an interest in astrology and somehow even psychology".

"Are you sure you want to work at an ad agency" – the abbot asked.

"I don't know" – I replied.

I had to admit I was average at everything and not a very creative person. Also I was not a very flamboyant person.

"What do I do" – I asked the abbot.

"Examine your competencies and know your weaknesses and then decide on the future course of action" – the abbot replied.

I was downcast and requested the abbot to suggest a course of action.

"Well," the abbot said, "you like astrology, psychology and like to research facts and at the same time you are slightly intuitive. Why don't you try your luck in the stock market".

"The stock market!" – I asked.

"People lose their life savings in the stock market. I've read a lot of horror stories in the papers" – I added.

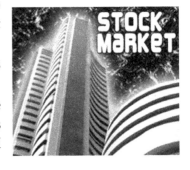

"Well I feel you will do well in that field" – the abbot added.

"Then the stock market is where my future lies" – I said.

I escorted the abbot to the living room where my parents and grandpa were waiting. I told them what the abbot had suggested as my future career option. My parents were delighted. My father knew a stock broker 'Search More and Sons' and promised to put in a word for me. 'Search More and Sons' was a small broking firm which had managed to do well because of their excellent client relations. In a time where all the small broking firms were either folding up or merging with bigger entities 'Search More and Sons' was thriving. I didn't care whether it was a large firm or a small firm I just wanted to learn. Meanwhile I informed Mr. Sathe at 'Rocking Kills' I would not be joining them. My dad soon fixed up an appointment with Mr. Tyagi a partner at 'Search More and Sons'.

The next afternoon I walked into the office of 'Search More and Sons'. It was a huge office, as big if not bigger than the office of 'Rocking Kills'. I asked Mr. Tyagi's secretary to inform Mr. Tyagi that I had arrived. I was ready to wait for an hour or so. After my experience at 'Rocking Kills', I was sure I would have to wait for at least an hour. I was wrong....

"There you are young man" – Came a loud cheerful voice.

Mr. Tyagi was a very tall man over six feet and very chubby. I reckoned he was at least 140 Kgs. He was bald. There was something very striking about Mr. Tyagi. He had a very broad smile and was very charming. He put me completely at ease within two minutes.

I got up from the sofa and smiled back at Mr. Tyagi. He caught hold of my hand and escorted me back to his cabin.

"You got 69%" he asked looking at my bio data.

"Yes Sir" - I replied. I thought probably my poor marks may become an issue.

"You spent one year at a monastery" – he asked.

"That's true Sir" – I replied.

"Wonderful" – came a loud cheerful reply.

"Do you know anything about stocks" – he asked.

"No Sir" – I replied.

"Why the stock market?" – he asked.

"Actually I wanted to work in an ad agency but the abbot of the monastery I lived in for one year suggested I try my luck in the stock market" – I replied.

"Are you bound by any precepts" – he asked.

"No sir I am not" – I replied.

"Good, this is the real world. I don't believe in right or wrong. I can't afford that luxury. Whatever is profitable is right. Money is my God. Do you understand?"

"Yes Sir" – I replied.

"Good, now I've even introduced you to my God" – he said laughing away.

"Of course, you are not expected to do anything wrong" – he added.

"There is lots you can do. You can choose to invest in shares or you can trade or you can do a bit of both. In that case I'm just adding a new client, not an apprentice. In case you want to have detailed knowledge of the market, then you can work in each and every department. I have an accounts section; demat department, compliance department, research department, client handling department (front office) and a small finance department. We are just 60 people so we have an HR team of only two people. Would you like to be an apprentice or a client?" – He asked.

"Sir, I would like to be an apprentice. I have college early morning, I can work afternoon onwards" – I replied.

"Good! You're hired! There is no stipend. I'll let you trade up to a small limit of Rs.two lacs every day without having to put up margin money" – he said.

"Why don't you borrow some money from your dad to invest in the market? It will be a good learning experience" – he added.

I nodded and understood Mr. Tyagi was of the shrewdest persons I had met. He had managed to get an apprentice working for free. I knew if I traded on shares I might make money or lose it, but Mr. Tyagi would only gain in the form of brokerage. Mr. Tyagi saw opportunity everywhere. This was in contrast to the closed minded creative people I experienced at the ad agency. I figured everything in this universe is not as it seems. May be the most creative, intuitive and open minded people actually headed for the stock market. They had to convert even disasters into opportunity.

I worked for a few weeks in every department of 'Search More and Sons'. It was almost six months since I had been working as an apprentice, but I neither traded nor made any investments. Mr. Tyagi and all the others thought I was plain scared. In truth I was neither scared nor risk averse. I was waiting for the right opportunity. The market was going nowhere. It had been in a tight range for months and

I figured the time was not right. Then all of a sudden one day it happened. The market rose over 4% on very heavy volumes. I checked the FII figures in the evening and the FII buying figure was huge. Foreign Investors had bought shares of nearly a billion dollars that day.

Mr. Tyagi smelt opportunity. He told everyone in the firm this was the time to sell. The next day we should all sell our holdings and in a few days the market would come

down. This seemed logical as there was no real news or reason for the rally. It looked like a stray one day movement in the market. I bunked college the next day and reached the firm early. Almost the entire staff had reached early so that they could short the market on the rise. I sat with Gloria, the chartist at the firm and tried to figure out where the opportunities lay.

Suddenly it struck me there was something wrong. The entire herd was ready to short sell that morning. But did the members of this herd determine stock prices? All the people around me were small fries. I had to think like the sharks. The market had been in a range for a very long time. The P/E ratios were on the lower side. If I bought shares at these rates, the downside was 3 to 4%, that's not much I thought. If I shorted shares at this level, I could gain 3 to 4% if I was right but I could lose 30 to 40% if I was wrong. I called up my dad and for the first time in six months asked him for some money to invest in shares.

Dad said "No problem take 10 lacs"

He was confident I must have done extensive research and must be convinced or he would never agree to give me such a large amount.

The truth was there was no research. It was just a hunch. I was behaving like a gambler. I bought four shares and invested 10 lacs that day. I was confident I was right even though everyone at the firm was betting on the market going to the bottom end of the range. The market closed another 4% higher that day and almost everybody at the firm closed their positions at a loss. Within a few days the trend was most decidedly upwards. In 4 months the market gained 50% and my portfolio was up 300%. My investment of 10 lacs was now worth 30 lacs. I repaid the 10 lacs my dad had given me and I had now a portfolio of 20 lacs. I was nearly 20 years old and had earned 20 lacs in the stock market in a few months. I was thankful I had not taken up the apprenticeship at 'Rocking Kills'. It was what I wanted. But sometimes it's good not to get what you want because something better may lie in store. I had made my first crore before my 21st birthday. It was not only about the money but I had won a lot of respect at home and with my friends. All my friend's parents soon started consulting me regarding their portfolios. This made me feel good. I was mostly conservative with their portfolios. Very soon even dad who believed in putting most of his money in fixed deposits with banks had the confidence to increase his exposure to the stock market. I didn't believe in putting my money anywhere other than in the stock market. But I was not looking at the markets with blinkers on. I knew there are periods of time when you should have the money anywhere other than the stock market.

"Even a fool makes money in a bull run. Those who survive the bear markets are the real players" – Mr. Tyagi often repeated.

I was making a lot of money in the market but in truth I was mentally preparing myself for my first bear run.

Would I be able to recognize the reversal of the trend? Would I be able to call correctly the start of the bear run?

I knew if I kept an open mind and didn't get carried away I would recognize the reversal of the trend. I just had to remember that just as night followed day, the bull market would be followed by a bear market. Only every time you looked at the screen you would reach the conclusion that a bear market is not possible any time soon. All TV channels were advising the list of stocks to be bought. Everyone I knew was talking about the amount of money others had made. The market kept going higher. I could make out there was a stock mania spreading across like wild fire. My intuition told me there was danger ahead, but still I resisted selling my portfolio. Since everybody was bullish I was keeping my eyes open. Oil was going higher, inflation and interest rates were going higher and the stock market was going higher.

Finally one day I had a terrible backache. I thought may be the sages were sending me a message and so I sold out my entire portfolio. I knew there was no message but a part of me told me, you never know!

Mr. Tyagi was surprised. He called me three times that day to inquire why I'd sold my portfolio.

I couldn't tell him I'd sold my entire portfolio on a hunch. So I told him the P/E ratios were very high and that in most cases the profits of the companies were unsustainable. Nothing happened in the market in the next one month. The market was up 7% that month and most people in the firm advised me to buy back my holdings. I decided to wait another month. Although the TV channels and newspapers were constantly discussing the rosy future that lies ahead, I was stubborn. Another month passed and the market was up another 5%. I decided to make a list of the stocks I wanted to buy. Everything was very expensive but was becoming even more expensive every passing day. I worked the whole night determined to invest my entire money in the stock market the next day. It was a Friday morning and I reached the office an hour before the market opened.

Mr. Tyagi walked into the office early and came up to me and asked me.

"How come you're so early?"

"Sir, I've decided to invest my money back into the market" – I replied.

"Good, make the best of the boom" – he replied.

"Don't be impulsive, take a second opinion" – he added.

I decided I'd wait a day or two, think things over and then invest.

There were no messages from the sages who had been my mentors. They never interfered with destiny.

After three days I invested a part of my spare money in the market. I did not know what lay ahead. I had decided I would send a part of my money to charities, the remaining money I would invest in the market. Soon I was fully invested. The bull run had lasted over four years now and this was my 5th year with the firm. My college was also over and very soon I would have to take a call on whether I wanted to do CA or MBA.

The market did crash when no one expected it do. Everyone was caught on the wrong foot including me. But I had a philosophy of stop losses. When the losses in the portfolio exceeded 20% I sold off my entire portfolio and put the money in Bank FD's. I was twenty three and now had over 10 crores in fixed deposits. All I had to do now was to wait out the bearish period and not be tempted to invest until the market stabilized. So I stopped going to the broking firm for more than an hour a day. Any way bear runs last a long time I figured. If I had to make a career in the stock markets I would have very little work and no source of income in bear periods. The stock market is brutal. You can make an obscene amount of money in bull runs and loose even your pants in the bear run. It was a business which had huge swings, very high highs and very low lows. "No body loses money in a bear market it's the bull run you have to survive" – Mr. Tyagi often said.

This was true. All reason and research is thrown out of the window in a bull run. The losses at the end of bull run are often non recoupable.

I decided it was time I met the sages again. So I asked my dad whether he would accompany me to the monastery.

I knew my dad would oblige. He was particularly proud of my success. I was not wrong – he told me he would call up the monastery and ask for an appointment with the abbot.

The abbot refused to give us an appointment. This was shocking.

I spent the next few days wondering why?

"We are so close, where is the distance? What is this need to meet physically" was the abbots' telepathic reply.

I perked up.

Ups and downs are a part of life. It's when the chips are down; you separate the men from the boys. A man's character is tested when the dice is loaded against him. You know who your friends are, when the times are tough.

I didn't know how long the bear run would last but I knew it wouldn't last forever. Nothing lasts forever.

And when the times changed I would be back. I had a gift, I always came back.

                                    The Perceptionist

The Decision

I decided it was time to do my MBA. My B.Com percentage had been a very good 87%. I had made a lot of money as a teenager by investing in the markets but my family valued education. If I had an MBA degree it would help in future if I  ever needed a job. Although I had tasted blood in the stock markets and was very sure there was no place else I intended to go. My vision was clear. I would learn everything that an MBA has to offer and then apply it in the stock market. The markets in India had opened up and foreigners from all over could invest in India. I was sure if India grew exponentially, in 20 years Indians would be investing money in markets all over the world. So I had to know everything connected with investing. I had to be the best in the trade. I wanted to earn a lot of money, not only for myself and my family but also for the causes I intended to support. Not many 24 year olds think of earning money so that they can support philanthropy. But I was different. Not many 24 year olds had lived for a year in a monastery. Not many 24 year olds had made crores in the stock market. Not many 24 year olds had received the blessings of the sages.

I cleared the MBA entrance tests effortlessly and got admission in a MBA College.

I badly wanted to take the blessings of the abbot and also of my gurus, Swami Ananddev and Swami Bholanath. So I broke all protocol and called up the abbot directly. The worst case scenario was that he would not take the call. It was as I thought; the abbot did not take my call. His assistant Sudha told me he was busy and would call back. I knew he would not call back. He did not call up anyone as a rule and he received only very urgent calls. I knew I shouldn't have called him up out of turn. But I longed to hear his voice. I was so busy in my thoughts that I did not hear my phone ringing. I saw the number on the phone - it was the abbot. My hand was shaking when I picked up the phone and in a faint voice, I said.

"Hello"

"Hari Om" –was the reply from the abbot, "you wanted to speak to me?"

"Yes Gurudev" – I replied.

"I've got admission in a MBA college and I wanted to give you the good news and take your blessings".

"My blessings are always with you" – came the booming reply.

"Come visit us any day of your choice" – the abbot continued.

This was great news. I had wanted to visit the monastery for a long time. Somehow I had never managed to get the permission to visit since a long time.

"Gurudev I will take the morning flight tomorrow and reach the monastery by afternoon tomorrow" – was my reply.

"Carry your clothes for a long stay, you may not return in a hurry" the abbot said before hanging up.

This was crazy. I had tried to go back to the monastery for the past 2-3 years but did not manage to get permission.

     The Perceptionist

Now that I had got admission into MBA and only wanted to have an overnight visit at the monastery, I was invited for a long stay. I had no clue as to what the abbot had on his mind. I spoke to my dad and did the bookings for the flight to Delhi and arranged for the car to take me to the monastery.

The flight was uneventful and I reached Delhi on time. Soon I was in the car on my way to the monastery. Life is totally unpredictable, when you have the answers ready life changes the questions. What does the abbot have on his mind? I wondered throughout the journey.

It was late afternoon when I reached the monastery. I immediately met Swami Sunil who worked as the manager at the monastery. I told him I didn't know how many days I would be staying at the monastery.

He allotted me a room temporarily so that I could put my luggage there and freshen up. I spend about five minutes in my room and then went to meet Sudha, the abbot's personal assistant. Sudha was a white robe wearer, who was always smiling and cheerful. I briefed her regarding my talk with the abbot and requested her to arrange a personal meeting with the abbot at the earliest. The abbot was resting so she asked to wait for some time.

I was a 24 year old who was eager to show off his spiritual knowledge. So I decided to test her knowledge. I asked her.

– "who are you"?

She smiled and did not bother to reply.

That deflated my ego. The white robe wearers at the monastery did not consider me worthy enough of sparring with me.

However I was not one to take that rejection seriously.

– "who are you"? I asked again.

"A seeker, just like you!" was her reply.

This made me even more confident. She was just a small assistant to the abbot whereas I had personally trained under the abbot and other gurus at the monastery. I had lived in the forbidden part of the monastery. I was special. I thought she definitely must be at the basic level whereas I was really advanced. I thought why not share a little bit of my knowledge with her. So I asked her.

– "what is your concept of God?"

She smiled even more and replied.

"I'm not yet advanced. God lies beyond the realms of the human mind. My mind has limitations. I couldn't possibly perceive God".

This was just like I thought; she was still at a basic level and had not reached a level where she could debate –the concept of God, which is the pinnacle of all thinking. Debating on the concept of God had blown many a mind. It can take you to a point logic and intuition cannot conceive.

"Send him in" – it was the abbot's voice.

I was led into the abbot's room and as soon as I saw the abbot I went forward to touch his feet. Sudha asked for permission to leave.

But the abbot said –

"Wait! I have a disciple for you"

This was crazy; the abbot wanted me at my very advanced level to learn from Sudha.

"Abbot Sir, she is a white robe wearer. I have studied under two orange robe wearers".

I said in a faint voice.

The abbot laughed loudly.

"What you should learn, only she can teach. Does the robe matter?"

"No! The robe does not matter."

I said in a faint voice.

The abbot looked at me sternly.

"Yes Gurudev! It matters to me. It should not. But it does" I replied truthfully.

"I thought she is a white robe wearer at my level. So how can she teach me"?

I said,

Both Sudha and the abbot had a hearty laugh.

"She wears a white robe because she feels it goes well with her complexion. She is qualified to wear the orange robe" was the abbots reply.

Clearly not everything was as it seems at the monastery. A white robe wearer turns out to be qualified to wear orange robes.

So how come I was allowed to stay in the forbidden part of the monastery for a year earlier, was it because I was special or was it because they thought I was 'dumbo', incapable of uncovering any secrets.

I had really lost a lot of my self confidence. May be I was not as special to the monks as I thought I was. May be I was not an advanced seeker. My doubts were set aside very quickly when I remembered I was in my early twenties and had a long way to go. I realized that besides being successful in life I was seeking something else also. It was not definable and I could not put my finger on it.

"So, what will Sudha ma'm be teaching me?" I asked.

"The art of deception" – The abbot replied.

The abbot got up and with a hand gesture indicated that the meeting was at an end. I got up, touched his feet, took his blessings and left the room along with Sudha.

Sudha ma'm escorted me to a teaching room which was just besides the abbot's room. My head was still spinning, what is this art of deception? Isn't it wrong to deceive? Isn't it wrong not to be truthful? I didn't know what to ask Sudha so I kept quiet.

"You will be required to stay for 40 days. Please inform your parents. I will make all the arrangements at the monastery. You can stay in the room you have been allotted at the monastery" – Sudha ma'm said.

"The art of deception is an ancient art. Deception is needed for survival. The human race would have perished long ago if we were incapable of deception. Right and wrong are a matter of perception. Time, place and circumstances could be such that it could be right to deceive. Have an open mind – it is possible that you are faced with circumstances where it is right to deceive" – Sudha ma'm continued.

I was not sure. I thought it was wrong to deceive.

"Have you read the Mahabharat" – ma'm asked.

I immediately remembered that even Lord Krishna had used deception in the war. I changed my tune. May be deception was not totally wrong.

"See how perception about right and wrong changes?" – Sudha ma'm asked.

I agreed with her. I was very negative about deception until I remembered Lord Krishna had used it to win the Mahabharat.

"All your life you decide what is right or wrong based on what others have told you. I want you to explore within yourself and tell me what you feel about deception" – ma'm asked.

"I feel it depends on the motive. In a war perhaps when the motive is survival, it is useful. In day to day life I am not so sure" – I replied.

"I know which of the students at the monastery is making progress and who is lying. I mingle among all the white robe wearers and they all share their problems with me. If I was wearing an orange robe would I know the problems faced by the white and yellow robe wearers? Of course, if I was wearing an orange robe I would get a lot more respect at the monastery, but I have sacrificed that respect and am moving around in a white robe so that the abbot knows accurately what is going on at the monastery. When you know your own self worth, you will not seek validation from others. So what do you think of my deception?

Sudha ma'm asked.

"Well you don't stand to gain anything from this deception. It is for the benefit of your students. I feel you should end it, and take the respect that an orange robe wearer gets" – I replied.

"Thank you for the offer. My self worth is not dependant on the colour of my robe. I really don't need reverence from others".

"We bother so much about what others think that we don't realize its immaterial. Our happiness should not be dependent on the opinion of others" – ma'm said in a pleasant voice.

"So will you study from me the art of deception over the next 40 days" – ma'm asked.

"Of course I will" – I replied.

"What if I tell all the others you are an orange robe wearer?" – I asked.

Ma'm laughed heartily.

"You won't, if you do tell them they won't believe you. They are influenced by what they see and hear".

That sealed the issue I was sure I won't tell anyone. It was late evening and Sudha ma'm asked me to see her in the teacher's room the next day at 9 a.m. All the white robe wearers at the monastery were addressed as swamis, only Sudha was called ma'm. This further gave the impression that she was not very advanced spiritually. But we all know that the truth was otherwise.

The next day I reached the teachers room sharp at 9 a.m. Sudha ma'm was there ready and smiling. I touched her feet and sat in front of her. This was the first time I had touched her feet and I felt very awkward. But the respect had to be given. Ma'm just smiled and acknowledged my mark of respect.

"So why do you think the abbot guided you to do something in the stock market. Why was he not keen that you become an apprentice at an Ad agency" – Sudha ma'm asked.

"I have no idea. He probably saw me earning a lot of money in the stock market. He probably saw the future" – I answered.

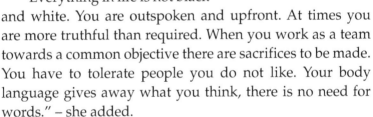

"No! It's because the stock market is an ideal place for individual brilliance. May be he was not sure how you would work as a team" – she said.

"So the abbot does not think I am a team player?" – I asked.

"Everything in life is not black and white. You are outspoken and upfront. At times you are more truthful than required. When you work as a team towards a common objective there are sacrifices to be made. You have to tolerate people you do not like. Your body language gives away what you think, there is no need for words." – she added.

"So I should use deceit?" – I asked her.

"If you want to live in a monastery, you are perfect as you are. However you come to the monastery with an objective to learn skills to succeed in life. To succeed in life you have to learn not to reveal more than what is required. You will have to master your body language and be very careful about what you say and to whom."

"But what do I do when I have to deal with say a difficult boss" – I asked.

"You learn to deal with him. Align your interests with his and you'll get off with him beautifully. See things from his point of view" – she replied.

"So you are teaching me life skills and not really deception" – I asked her.

"You can word it any way you want, the substance remains the same. The universe is a web of self interests. Your self interest first, then that of your family, then state, then country, then continent and then your planet, your universe and so on. Everybody thinks more or less in the same way. This is valuable knowledge, exploit it" – Sudha ma'm said.

"I don't know how to" I replied.

"It's simple. People first represent themselves or family in any business deal. If they grow bigger they start representing their state, then their country and so on" ma'm explained.

I was not catching the drift. So I truthfully said.

"Ma'm, I didn't understand."

"What to do with you? You're supposed to say – ma'm, you're a brilliant teacher, I understand!" ma'm said laughing away.

"In a life situation you are supposed to tell people what they want to hear. If your boss has taken a decision and then he asks you your opinion, you are expected to agree with him. If he asks you before he takes the decision you have to estimate from his body language what he wants to hear. You cannot wander around telling people home truths. If you want to be truthful, be truthful to yourself. In a real situation you will have a few truths to say about everybody and that will make you extremely unpopular. If you want to be truthful you can either stay at the monastery or engage in a business activity where you need individual brilliance" ma'm added.

The first lesson was drawing to a close. Soon I was back in my room pondering on what was taught. It was apparent to me that I had grown up in a protected environment. I had no idea of how the sharks operated in the real world. I had made a lot of money in the stock market but that was due to my individual brilliance. I had not really set up an organization. If I wanted to do my MBA and set up a big organization, I would have to deal with people. All types of people. Apparently individual brilliance would not be enough. I needed acute people skills. I had to hire a lot of brilliant people and see that they were happy and motivated. I had to make them believe my success was their success. Not all the people I hired would be ethical, I had to learn to tolerate their lies and not show my true feelings. I would have to see that they did not digress from my overall vision and ethics. I could see that I was already planning something big after my MBA. I knew that when the time was ripe, the big idea would come. The excitement was so high that I didn't sleep all night.

I reached the teachers room sharp at 9 a.m. the next morning. I touched Sudha ma'm's feet and sat before her.

"You are excited" – Sudha ma'm said.

"I didn't sleep. I was planning to launch a big company after my MBA. I need your blessings and I know my dreams will come true" – I said.

"Some dreams had better not come true. Your dreams are relatively small. I pray your dreams come true" – Sudha ma'm said.

"The topic for today is self. You can be happy only if you understand yourself and what motivates you. So what motivates you?" Ma'm asked.

"Although I am in my early twenties, you know I have done well for myself in the stock market. I think creating something would motivate me. Alternatively doing something for society would also motivate me. May be money would not motivate me as much as it motivates others. But then you never know. May be I will find someone

 The Perceptionist

exciting in my MBA class and everything I say today would be thrown out of the window" I replied.

"So maybe you will find love on the horizon" – Sudha ma'm said.

"You never know" – was my reply.

"So will you bring her to the monastery" – ma'm asked.

"Yes, hopefully she will be as excited about visiting the monastery as I am" – I replied.

"Where will you find an attractive young girl who is spiritually inclined?" – ma'm asked.

"Hopefully in my MBA class" – was my reply.

The session ended on a light note. I went back to my room to complete the introspection and contemplation exercises that were given to me. I decided to attend the dinner ceremony held at the monastery. I normally had only fruits for dinner, and I preferred to have the fruits in my room. Dinner at the monastery was a solemn affair. Monks stood in their specially assigned places and chanted some mantras. The guests had specifically assigned places. After the mantras were chanted everybody sat down. After the abbot had tasted the first morsel, everyone started eating. Normally the yellow robe bearers had the privilege of serving food. The food at the monastery was awful. There was very little salt and no spices or oil used in the cooking. I was really hungry so I ate up all the food served to me. I obviously refused the second helping offered to me. No one spoke; there was almost pin drop silence for 10 minutes. Once the abbot was through, he got up and everyone followed. I made my way to my room.

"What are you learning here?" – a voice asked.

I turned around. It was an elderly looking gentleman in his sixties.

I didn't know what to say.

"Sudha ma'm is teaching me the art of deception" – I replied truthfully.

"Why are you lying?" he asked.

It was obvious he didn't believe me.

"Actually it's not deception she's teaching me. She's teaching me how to deal with others and introspect about myself" – I replied.

This was more believable, but he still couldn't figure out what this had to do with spirituality.

"Since I'm very young she's giving me basic life skill lessons. Mantras and other higher teaching are imparted to older people who can grasp it better" – I added.

He was very pleased. He told me he had been given a mantra and also permission to stay at the monastery for full two months to practice the same. I did not reveal to him that I had been given a mantra long back and had practiced it for over a year at the monastery. Clearly I had made a friend at the monastery. Had I boasted, I would have felt good but not made a friend. I went to my room and decided to tuck in for the night.

Soon I heard a knock on the door. It was my newly found friend Mr. Kumar. He was standing outside my room with two huge bars of chocolates.

"These are for you" – Mr. Kumar said handing me over his two chocolates bars.

"I can't accept them" – I replied.

"Nonsense! You are my grandson's age, you can't say no to chocolates" he said putting the two bars in my hand.

There was also a chit of paper on top of the two bars.

"What's in this chit sir? – I asked.

"Oh, I've jotted down my mantra for you to practice. It is a secret mantra; I can give it to members of my family to practice. If you practice this mantra long enough you will find what you truly seek. None of the members of my family would take the time out to practice a mantra or visit a monastery. I guess you are my true family. I'm sure you will practice the mantra." – Mr. Kumar said.

गुरुर्ब्रह्मा गुरुर्विष्णुः गुरुर्देवो महेश्वरः ।
गुरुः साक्षात् परं ब्रह्म तस्मै श्री गुरवे नमः ॥

All I had done was to give Mr. Kumar a little bit of respect and love and he was ready to go out of his way to help me. Had I showed off my attainments and put him down, I would not have found a friend, Sudha ma'm was right. I could speak the truth but judiciously. Instead of finding a lot of things to criticize in others, I could always find a thing or two to praise in people. And I could still stick to speaking the truth.

"How many times should I practice this mantra." – I asked Mr. Kumar.

He turned and smiled.

"If the abbot gives you his blessings, a 100 times a day will suffice."

"You will experience something mystical which only the lineage has to offer."

I went forward and touched his feet.

"I will practice this mantra with your blessings. How many times will suffice?"

I expected him to say 10,000 or 50,000. After all he was of a far lower rank than the abbot.

He smiled and said –"with my blessings you need not practice this mantra. I will transfer the experience to you."

I was shocked. How could Mr. Kumar be more powerful than the abbot?

"You hid things from me about your attainments, so I did the same. I have practiced this mantra millions of times. I can gift you the experience. It's no big deal" – Mr. Kumar said.

"What will I experience?" – I asked.

"Nothing!" – Mr. Kumar replied.

"Nothing?" – I repeated.

"Nothing that can be described using words. You will be able to smell out the truth, you will always know where the truth lies." – Mr. Kumar said.

I closed the door and went to sleep. The next morning I reached a little early. I touched ma'm's feet and sat in front of her for the next lesson.

"So why are you beaming?" – Sudha ma'm asked.

"I made a friend at the monastery" – I replied.

"Who?" – ma'm asked.

"Mr. Kumar, he gave me chocolates and a mantra to practice." – I replied.

"There is no guest by that name at the monastery" – she replied.

"Are you hallucinating?"

"No! I just ate the two chocolate bars he gave me yesterday night. I have the mantra also written down on a piece of paper" – I replied.

"What was the mantra he gave you? Ma'm asked."

"Guru Brahma, Guru Vishnu, Guru devo............I have forgotten the mantra but I have it on a piece of paper" – I replied.

"Oh! Don't bother it's from the Guru Gita" – she said.

"Did he say anything else?" – she asked.

"He said if the abbot blessed me, 100 times a day would suffice for a mystical experience. And that if he blessed me he could just transfer the experience to me" – I replied.

"That was Param Guru Jaidev. The abbot's guru. It is his mantra you were referring to. No one but Param Guru Jaidev can transfer the experience effortlessly." – ma'm said.

It was clear to me that Sudha ma'm was really excited. Having a vision of Param Guru Jaidev was regarded as a very big achievement. Here I had not only had a vision of Param Guru Jaidev but he had also passed on to me a mantra. Also Param Guru Jaidev's full name was Kumar Jaidev, so he had not lied when he told me his name was Kumar.

"So what mantra do I practice when I go home?" – I asked ma'm.

I asked because I had earlier been given a mantra by the abbot. I practiced that mantra diligently.

"Drop everything else and practice the mantra given to you by Param Guru Jaidev. He would know best what is good for you. We have manuscripts to help us decipher which way the future will unfold. You have visited the secret chambers on an earlier visit. To decipher the truth it is important to have clear perception. I will not lie to you. I saw very clearly in my visions when I visited the chamber that you would be cheated several times over. You are just not worldly wise. So I decided to give you classes on deception. The abbot also agreed you are not worldly wise and it would be good if we showed you the face of truth. The visions are never wrong so what we saw was probably true but not material enough to affect your life adversely. May be I did not see far enough in the future. I will revisit the chamber and then decide whether you need any further classes from me. Besides Param Guru Jaidev has walked into your life. This changes everything. Your life may change materially. Other than the abbot, I don't know anyone who has ever had a vision of Param Guru Jaidev. He does not go around giving a mantra on a chit to youngsters, you know" Sudha ma'm replied.

"Take the day off, while the abbot and I decide what is to be done with you." were ma'm's instructions.

I decided to attend the dinner ceremony again. This time when the mantras were being read, I was looking around trying to spot Mr. Kumar. Once the abbot had the first morsel everyone started with their food. The food was awful again. Everyone ate in silence and once the abbot got up everyone disbursed to go to their rooms. I went towards my room slowly. Hoping to meet Mr. Kumar or Param Guru Jaidev again. Nothing is mystical happened and soon I was sleeping in my room.

I went to meet Sudha ma'm early in the morning at 9 a.m. as per my daily schedule. I touched her feet and sat before her; she motioned me to get up and led me to the abbots' chamber.

The abbot looked at me and smiled.

"So my Guru has visited you lately?" – the abbot asked.

I didn't know what to say so I remained silent.

"Was there any instructions given on how to practice the mantra"? – he asked.

"No!" – I replied.

"Did he give you any practices to do before or after you recite the mantra?" – he asked again.

"No!" – I replied.

"Did he give you any precepts?

"No!" – I replied.

"So you only recite the mantra?" – the abbot asked.

"Yes!" I replied.

"Was there any phrase or set of words he gave you to use as a password before you recite the mantra"? the abbot asked.

"No!" – I replied.

"Why you?" – The abbot asked.

"He said he could give it to members of his family to practice. He felt that the members of his family would not take the time out to practice the mantra" – I replied.

"I am unable to access your past beyond this lifetime. It has been blocked. Or I would easily prove to you that you don't deserve Param Guru Jaidev's vision. There is nothing remarkable about your future. So why you?" – The abbot asked.

"Nothing is as it seems" – I replied.

The abbot was concerned. He was the transmitter for a very authentic lineage. He did his work meticulously and with a great deal of dedication. Deserving students were always given priority. He had put me on low priority for the last four years because he felt my Karmas were not spectacular or deserving. Now he was confused. Why had his Guru intervened? He and his Guru had the same information regarding my Karmas. His Guru's perception regarding the Karmas was different. I guess Param Guru Jaidev did not believe in a fixed concept of wrong or right. He was very flexible. Though the abbot was doing his job with utmost diligence, there was need for intervention by a higher authority. This showed me that no one is perfect. You could have access to all the facts and yet make a gross miscalculation.

"Param Guru Jaidev is never wrong. I respect his decision. I will help you make progress" – the abbot said.

"There are certain practices you must undertake before you do japa of the mantra that was given to you. There is a password for the mantra also. I will teach you both. It is clear that you are ready" – the abbot added.

The abbot spent the next two hours teaching me everything I must know before I practiced the mantra.

When I had learnt the practices and the password and the abbot was satisfied, he asked me to go to my room and rest. He would call for me if I was needed again. It was late evening when Swami Shiva came to my room and informed me that I must meet the abbot the next day at 10 a.m. I chit chatted with Swami Shiva for some time about the going on at the monastery. I asked him about my case and my vision of Param Guru Jaidev. Swami Shiva was not of much help there. Only the orange robe wearers would know, he informed me. I decided to skip dinner and retire early.

The next morning I reached the abbot's chamber at 10 a.m. sharp. He was waiting for me. I touched his feet and sat in front of him.

"You have spent nearly a week at the monastery, so how was your stay?" – he asked.

"It was good!" – I answered.

"There is no need for you to stay here for 40 days. You can leave today or tomorrow. There is nothing you need to learn. Just practice the mantra that was given to you. God bless you!" – the abbot said.

"I will follow your instructions" – I replied.

The abbot made a hand gesture and I knew the meeting was over. I returned to my room and arranged for a car to take me to the airport. I was lucky I managed to get the ticket for the evening flight to Mumbai. I packed my clothes and waited for the car to arrive at the monastery. When my car arrived at the monastery I immediately put my bag in the car and went to Sudha ma'm's chamber to wish her farewell. She was heading for the meditation chambers as it was time for the group meditation at the monastery. I touched her feet and she gave me her blessing. I hurried and met the abbot before he was about to enter the meditation chamber. He gave me his blessing and asked me to practice diligently. Soon I was in the car heading for the airport. My flight was on time and I reached Mumbai at night. Soon I was home,

                                    The Perceptionist

briefing my parents about what happened at the monastery. My father advised me to practice the mantra diligently. I assured him I would. Anyway the timing was perfect, my MBA classes started the day after. If I would have stayed in the monastery for 40 days I would have missed at least one month of my MBA. I decided I would rest and laze around the next day and mentally prepare for my life's most important degree.

The MBA Classes Began

I reached the MBA College an hour early. Dad had gifted me a brand new Alto. It was a really sleek car. So with all the confidence in the world I made my way into the introductory lecture in the auditorium. I decided it would be safer not to sit right in the front, so I went and sat in the 8th row. Very soon the other students started streaming in. The dress code was formal so I guess everybody looked far smarter than usual. Very soon a very tall and lanky young man came and sat next to me. He was very fair and exuded confidence. I smiled at him and introduced myself. He smiled back and gave me his name – Vikas. He had done his engineering and worked with a Tata company for two years. He now wanted to build on his qualifications by doing MBA and further his job prospects. In the break I met several of my classmates. Most of my classmates were from Mumbai, but there were a few from out of town. They were either staying with relatives or had made hostel or paying guest arrangements. I soon became friends with Vijay. He had a background just like mine. He was passionate about the stock market and was determined to apply everything he learnt here later on in life. We spent endless hours discussing plans of making it big in the stock market. We had understood that there were patterns to life. If you could identify the patterns you could make a fortune. We understood algorithmic trading was based on this. Identify patterns and back test their effectiveness. Since I had made a lot of money in the market, I had purchased a Monte Carlo simulator for my simulations. Vijay suggested that we should try for an apprenticeship with some foreign firms, so that we would have industry experience along with our MBA. We both thought about it but than decided against it. The pressure of assignment and presentations was too high. So we decided we would do the apprenticeship during our summer vacations like everyone else. There were several investment banks visiting our campus and we decided we would try our luck only with the top investment banks. Vijay was really smart and had crafted a fantastic resume. In his other interests he had mentioned that he was excellent at chess. This was to impress his interviewers regarding his analytical abilities. I thought of mentioning chess in my resume but then decided against it. I was no good at chess and if the interviewer pulled out a chess board I would be badly exposed. I mentioned my experience at the monastery and thought this was a big USP that I had, if the interviewers had an open mind.

As I thought Vijay's interview with Silver Ox did not go to well. Silver Ox was the world largest investment bank and they paid five times what the normal investment banks paid. They naturally had the best talent working for them. The moment Vijay started boasting about his chess skills, they pulled out a chess board out of nowhere and asked him to take on a member of their interviewing panel. Vijay was no match and didn't get the apprenticeship. In life it pays to create a hype only around good products. Vijay had briefed me about his interview so; I was relatively prepared for mine.

I had decided I would definitely not mention that I played chess. But the first query I faced was.

"Don't you play chess?"

I replied – "A little but I'm not good at it"

"If you are no good at chess, how can you be good at analyzing information and being ahead of others?" – they asked.

"A chess player has to follow the rules of the game. Life has no rules. You can choose to have an open mind and not be bound by anything. The best response in real life is usually the one that's spontaneous" – I replied.

"You're hired!"

Was the response of the elderly gentleman on the panel. I found out later, he was a partner at Silver Ox.

I was thrilled. There were several investment banks which would be visiting the campus but none were spoken in the same breath as Silver Ox. If you worked for Silver Ox, you were good. Silver Ox was a treasure house for talent. They recruited experts from several fields, even scientists and sportsmen and applied their expertise to make money in the markets. The expert analysts at Silver Ox often knew as much or more about the product than the companies producing and selling the product. I knew all I had was a summer internship and you cannot learnt much in two months but I wanted to make these two months count. These two months could be a life changer for me. I was eager to learn. I knew that the summer interns at Silver Ox were supposed to make a presentation at the end of two months. If I made an impression, there's no way they would not recruit me during the final placement rounds. Meanwhile Vijay got his summer internship offer from Make My Day Investments. They were very impressed with his insights and also his preparation for the interview. Both of us started our respective internships.

My first day at Silver Ox was an unforgettable experience. I walked in formally dressed unsure about how things would shape up. As soon as I reached Silver Ox at 9.30 a.m. I was received by Shriya. Shriya was Mr. Grey's secretary. Mr. Grey was the partner who had decided to recruit me. She told me Mr. Grey would see me in 10 minutes and I made myself comfortable in the space outside Mr. Grey's cabin. Very shortly Mr. Grey came out to see me and escorted me into his cabin. He ordered some coffee for me and his body language indicated he was in no hurry to end the meeting.

"So you have travelled extensively?" – he asked.

"Yes Sir, mainly US and Europe" – I replied.

"So which country did you like?" he asked.

"I loved The Vatican and Paris" I replied.

"What did you like in both these places?" he asked.

"Art" – I replied.

I spent the next 10 minutes explaining how fascinating I found The Vatican and also the art in the museums in Paris.

"So you have good taste" – Mr. Grey said.

"What specific area would you want to cover for your summer assignment?" – Mr. Grey asked.

I had brought specific alternatives of companies and industries I intended to research but at the last minute I went by my gut feel and went for something totally different.

"I would like to research human perception" – I said.

"What?" Mr. Grey said.

I explained to Mr. Grey that value of art was just a matter of perception. I spent a few hours before the portrait of Monalisa wondering how it could be priceless. But I dare not voice my opinion before anybody because they would feel I didn't understand art. Everybody loved the Monalisa because everybody else loved it.

"How will you connect your research with the stock market and make money for us?" – Mr. Grey asked.

I explained to him that the prices of stocks were a function of perception. Some stocks never got P/E ratio over 2 or 3 while others got crazy P/E ratio of over 100. Everything was perception. If only we knew how human perception worked we could make trillions.

Mr. Grey looked at me and laughed.

"You would like to research human perception and connect it up with the markets; I will call you Mr. P from now on. It's short for 'The Perceptionist'." – Mr. Grey said.

I didn't like to be called Mr. P but my stint with Sudha ma'm had convinced me that I must get along with people.

"I'd love to be called Mr. P" – I replied.

"If you can deliver a decent report you can holiday in Paris as long as you like at the expense of Silver Ox" – Mr. Grey said.

The first part was easy. I had a project to work on. It was an unusual subject but I knew the partners at Silver Ox took a deep interest in unusual subjects. Anything outside of normal was an opportunity. I went back to my desk ready to list out the areas I would need to cover. All of a sudden Shriya's voice jolted me out of my deep thoughts.

"Boss feels you should have that cabin" – Shriya said.

She was pointing to Mr. Dutta's cabin. Mr. Dutta was on a long leave of over two months. He had been an out standing performer for several years and so had decided to take a long vacation and get to know his family better. I was overjoyed. I now had my own cabin at Silver Ox and I was just a summer intern.

The two months went off well. I conducted my research in an organized and methodical manner. I listed out several companies which had begun small and then grown very big where investors had made a lot of money. I was looking for patterns. I was looking for what all these companies had in common. On the exterior there was nothing in common. But I could not help noticing as the sample got bigger the pattern got clearer. In every company the only thing that mattered was the people. Everything else could be bought. Technology could be replicated. Bigger plants could be set up in no time. The only thing that can't be bought is vision. After several days of debating and analyzing every factor that had contributed, I narrowed down to the one most important factor. Only the quality of management and the people they are capable of recruiting mattered in my final analysis. My presentation went off very well and my report was appreciated by Mr. Grey.

"It is a good effort but it's not knocked me senseless. I thought you would come up with something sensational which would force me to give you a job offer today. You should have forced me to give you a letter today even though your MBA ends a year later." Mr. Grey said.

"True Sir but sometimes the truth lies in front of us and yet we are not able to see it" I replied.

"Enlighten me" Mr. Grey said.

"Everyone knows that people are the most important resource but few capitalize on it. How many organizations are people friendly and among them how many give a scope to their employees to be creative. Several companies I have met have no vision. They talk of numbers over the next 5 years but they have no vision. They are in it to make money. It makes no difference to them whether they make toys or socks" I replied.

"Go on" Mr. Grey said.

"If I was to make shoes I would be spending a huge amount on research. Not only about the colours and cut of the shoes but about the experience. I would want to create a brand loyalty. I would want customers to take pride in wearing my brand of shoes. Above all I would want my shoes to be most comfortable because that is why shoes were created. Because walking bare feet is not a comfortable experience" – I added.

"So vision is important everyone knows that" – Mr. Grey said.

"Yes Sir, it's an indefinable quality. But I have visited companies as a summer intern and I could make out where the promoters had a spark. Passion cannot be hidden" – I said.

"So to detect the passion and vision we will need you" – Mr. Grey asked.

"No Sir! You can use your experience. I have listed several factors which are important in my report" – I said.

"That's good all the VP's are assembling in the board room after an hour. We will debate your report threadbare, why don't you join us" – Mr. Grey said.

I didn't know if I was to participate and defend my findings or just sit and watch. I reached the board room 10 minutes early and sat behind my name plate. I got up and wished each of the VP's who entered the room. Each of them had been given a copy of my report in advance. All the VP's took turns to give me their insights and suggestions. Only Mr. Roy asked me a direct question.

"Why this interest in human perception?"

"It came to me on the spur of the moment when I was talking to Sir" – I replied.

"Clearly you are brilliant, I have never pondered on perception and its effect on stock market prices. To do an organized research paper on it as a summer intern is brilliant." – Mr. Roy added.

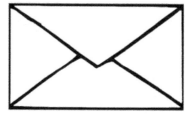

Clearly Mr. Grey was thrilled. After all I was his find. He proudly handed over an envelope to me. The envelope had tickets to Paris for me and a cheque to cover all the expenses for over a month.

"I think if you spend more time in museums in Paris you may get more ideas to continue your research when you join us at the end of your MBA." – Mr. Grey said.

I was thrilled I had an all expenses paid trip to Paris and an offer to join Silver Ox after my MBA.

"Look around you in the board room" – Mr. Grey said.

"The people around you are the best. They are deeply passionate about what they do. Throughout my life I have done only one thing and that is to recruit the best and then give them scope to thrive." – Mr. Grey said.

"If you had used the parameters of my report 20 year back on your investment bank it was possible to predict your success" – I added.

"You have a spark kid, you'll go a long way Mr. P" – Mr. Grey said.

I walked out of Silver Ox that day a satisfied young man. I had an offer from the world's best investment bank a year before I completed my MBA. Silver Ox had never recruited anyone average. Clearly I was not average anymore. What had the sages done?

I had changed. A transformation had taken place yet, it was the same face in the mirror. I was the same and yet I was different. The trust my parents had in the sages was not belied. The sages had done their job.

I was now called Mr. P at Silver Ox. We all know that's short for 'The Perceptionist'.

CPSIA information can be obtained
at www.ICGtesting.com
Printed in the USA
BVHW051122060321
601818BV00011BA/1586